SAVING AVA

WHEN POLITICAL POWER AND INSATIABLE GREED DECIDES WHO LIVES AND DIES.

ANNA CHAMBERS

DEFIANCE PRESS
& PUBLISHING

SAVING AVA

DEFIANCE PRESS
& PUBLISHING

ISBN-13: 978-1-963102-27-7 (Paperback)
ISBN-13: 978-1-963102-26-0 (eBook)

Published by Defiance Press & Publishing, LLC

Cover Design by Anna Chambers

Bulk orders of this book may be obtained by contacting Defiance Press & Publishing, LLC. www.defiancepress.com.

Public Relations Dept. – Defiance Press & Publishing, LLC
281-581-9300
pr@defiancepress.com

Defiance Press & Publishing, LLC
281-581-9300
info@defiancepress.com

DEDICATION

This book is dedicated to my children. May you know that my
relentless drive to push forward when life is hard has always been
powered by my unwavering love and commitment to all three of you.
It has been the greatest joy of my life to be your mom.

ACKNOWLEDGMENTS

I would like to acknowledge every single person who has played a hand in shaping my life. There are not enough pages in this book to include everyone who touched my heart along the way with their kindness. I couldn't begin to adequately thank you all. I would also like to thank the people who didn't help—the people who judged, were too afraid to speak the truth, doubted me, unfriended me, or thought I was crazy. Without me witnessing your censorious behavior firsthand, I wouldn't have learned the lessons in life that have made me into the woman I am today. A woman I am immensely proud of. I will forever be indebted to you. I know that God will continue to use me as a vessel to preach the truth and to never stop digging to find the root cause of illness. The betrayals and injustice I have endured ignited a fire in me that will only continue to grow. I forgive anyone who has ever done me wrong, as you will one day be judged for the choices you made in life. And I will continue to use the voice that you helped empower to inspire others.

TABLE OF CONTENTS

A MEMOIR

Pushing back on the norm, following my gut, and changing the narrative; navigating as a caregiver through life's curveballs, my way.

I bathed Ava as she sat naked in the shower, pale, weak, and barely a shell of who she once was just a few years back. I circled her back gently with the soapy loofa, washed her fragile body, and shampooed what was left of her hair. She allowed this just as she had once done as a small child, with zero concern for modesty. This alone is a red flag for a teenage girl. Now, there was nothing behind what used to be her bright-blue eyes when I looked into them. They were lifeless and dull, and it shook me to my core. These were the nights I would wake to check on her, like I had done when she was a baby, to make sure she was still breathing.

She had cut off her long, thick, beautiful blonde hair and dyed it black with box hair dye she had ordered without my permission. She had her own money and debit card. She had started her first job, working at a pet store, but was forced to quit when the pain got to be so much that she needed to be admitted.

Ava had always been known for her hair, even as a child. It would curl in the Florida humidity where she was born, and it grew long and thick as she got older. She was the lucky one who inherited my mom's gorgeous locks. It was about three times the normal amount of hair a person has, and twice as thick. It was naturally blonde with streaks of almost white.

As a former hairstylist, I internally cringed at this new look she had given herself, but at the time, that was the least of my worries.

Her hair had thinned a lot when she started taking immunosuppressants for an autoimmune disorder she was previously diagnosed with. I think at the time, she was going through a rebellious self-discovery phase, or perhaps she was secretly afraid of the clumps of hair she'd seen daily in the shower after washing it. She had also just returned from a three-week inpatient pain program that I would later learn filled her head with bizarre possible explanations for her pain. I eventually would realize this program was the biggest scam of her life, and mine. What we had thought was going to be a way out of her pain was truly the beginning of a rapid decline.

She looked unkempt and unclean, and it bothered me. Finally, I asked if she would like me to help her. She seemed surprised. It was my friend Roxanne, a nurse practitioner, who suggested that maybe Ava needed me to do things for her that I did not even need to do for her as a young child.

This went against everything I was told to do by the experts at the pain clinic. I wasn't supposed to ask her about her pain, or ask her if she needed help. I hadn't yet discovered that she was also told not to talk to me about her pain, or even to mention it. I would later realize that this brainwashing gave the program some pretty good success rates online. That success rate was what had given me the push to send her after it was recommended by what I once believed was a world-renowned hospital. I still feel guilty—for being so desperate to find answers that I took the advice of people who not only didn't help her, but also misdiagnosed and prolonged her physical and mental suffering, to put it mildly.

Roxanne had personally witnessed Ava deteriorating for a while. She worked from a very scientific perspective and would typically align with what Ava's doctors were telling me. But when she saw something that frightened her, something unusual, it shook me. Roxanne did not get rattled often, and seeing her this way left me so unsettled. She worked with very sick transplant patients and had seen it all, and she was typically unfazed. It had been a bit since she had physically seen Ava. When she watched her attempt to walk down the stairs—gripping the railing, her legs awkwardly shifting like they would buckle at any moment as she attempted each step, grimacing, withdrawn, and pale—her eyes grew wide. She saw a girl who was truly struggling and needed help with the most basic of things.

Before we became friends, I would watch Roxanne from my kitchen window while doing my dishes. She would run endless hours of basketball and baseball drills in her front yard with her two boys. She was a sports-loving, basketball-shorts-wearing boy mom; I was not. When I watched her in motion from afar, she even moved in a very masculine way. It wasn't until I really looked at her up close that I realized how beautiful, petite, and feminine she was.

I had never felt like we would have much in common because we seemed so different. The years would prove me wrong, though, and I only wish I would have known her sooner. I like to tell her I think she has the brain of a man, if that makes any sense. If you ever need to know what your husband is thinking, you ask Roxanne. You could put the exact same scenario in front of us and we would see it in completely different ways, but we always want the same outcome. This was often helpful when I needed someone to listen to the roadblocks I was having with Ava's healthcare and provide another perspective.

Roxanne worked in the hospital where Ava stayed for ten days two years ago when she was initially diagnosed with ulcerative colitis a few months after having Covid. Rox would force me out of her room, assuring me the nurses would keep a good eye on her for the time it took for me to have a cup of coffee and go for a short walk. Ava didn't get to finish school that year, either. Her eighth-grade year ended early due to Covid, and she spent the end of her freshman year of high school in the hospital. It was a scary time, similar to the year prior, but in a different way. Little did I know that the real nightmare was just beginning.

That was a very stressful time for me. I was diving into research, changing Ava's diet, and trying to take control of this horrible illness. Roxanne would remind me when I was getting a little crazy and force me out of my comfort zone. My comfort zone was my house, where I spent hours hovering over every little detail. Forcing me out of it typically meant having two drinks at a bar a mile away once a month. Even though our friendship consists mostly of spontaneous cups of coffee on the patio midday before the buses come, Rox knew I needed to physically get out of my house. It sounds silly, but you'd laugh if you knew just how much I resisted and how persistent she was. I'm grateful for her relentlessness.

"Can I help you shampoo your hair, Ava?" I quietly asked. "Shave your legs for you?" Her lifeless eyes looked up at me and nodded yes. That day, I washed my seventeen-year-old's body in the bathtub, shaved her legs, and shampooed her hair. I dried her off and held her weak body under her elbow as I helped her back to her room. I put lotion on her arms, legs, and feet, which had scars on top of them from the constant itching, and helped her get dressed. She looked up at me with grateful eyes and said, "I just don't have the energy to do it." It was heartbreaking. I had taken her to every specialist, multiple times, with zero answers. I had never felt so helpless. It was my job to advocate for her, to get answers, and relief, but I was failing miserably.

Ava had been experiencing unexplained symptoms that doctors didn't think had anything to do with her inflammatory bowel disease, or the medication she was taking. But the secondary symptoms had slowly started a few months after starting immunosuppressant medications, and it was baffling to me. She had chronic leg pain and tingling feet. She was sleeping any chance she got. Her heart would race for no reason. She was passing out. She was having chronic bloody noses and rashes. Her hair was falling out, and she had severe brain fog. She went from using a cane to a walker and finally a wheelchair, all with zero explanation from medical professionals. She missed over three hundred hours of school her junior year of high school.

She had already been through so much, and it seemed unfair we were now facing yet another obstacle, one I feared could take her from me completely if we didn't find answers soon. I thought a genetic disorder, multiple surgeries, the tragic death of her father, and moving across the country all before the age of five seemed unfathomable, but the world, for some reason, didn't think she was done, and neither was I.

The day I bathed her, I talked to my sister, Kelly, and told her I felt like Ava was dying right in front of my eyes. I had taken her to every doctor, every specialist multiple times, and no one was helping. This was the day I finally realized I would have to take matters into my own hands. Whatever I was doing was not working, and I internally felt like we were running out of time. No one was coming to save us, so I made her a promise that I would save her myself. I promised that I would not give up until I figured it out, and there wasn't a person or obstacle on this earth that would stop me.

"I'm not getting any responses," said the audiologist. "She is profoundly deaf in both ears."

Hearing aids were suggested, and I vaguely remember the words "cochlear implant" being said somewhere in the middle of my fog of shock. Her father got in his car to head back to work, and Ava and I got in mine. I headed back to our new apartment, where I knew no one.

I thought of all the times I had tried to soothe her with my voice or a song. I thought back on my pregnancy when I had played music for her inside me and talked to her, relishing in the miracle of how she would already know my voice when she was born and be comforted just by the sound of it. She cried on the way home that day in her rear-facing car seat, not able to see my face. It hit me then that she had never been comforted by my voice, and maybe never would be. I stretched my hand as far back as I could, hooking my pinky finger into her mouth as I drove, and she instantly calmed. Everything I had been taught about motherhood and caring for a newborn was about to change. I was heading into uncharted waters without a compass, and I was scared.

We had just moved to Florida for part of my husband's pilot training in the military. We lived in an apartment off base, and because official training had not started, I hadn't had the opportunity to meet any friends yet. Typically in the military, the families and wives come together quickly to welcome new people and are especially catering toward pregnant ones about to welcome their first baby. I didn't have this luxury, however, as the timing of our move and due date was odd.

I caught my husband at a light where I had to turn left and he, right. He looked over at me with tears in his eyes and mouthed, "I'm sorry."

I thought that would be our worst of life's curveballs. It wasn't. He just wouldn't be alive to hear the news that his daughters could also be losing their sight.

After suffering a miscarriage with my first pregnancy, I was over the moon ecstatic when I finally reached the twelve-week mark with the next pregnancy, and everything looked perfect. I was so careful—I did everything I was supposed to do and nothing I wasn't. I hung on every word my doctors said and prided myself on creating the perfect home for my little one to grow.

After realizing that my husband started flight training on her due date, we spoke with the doctor, and without hesitation he said, "We can induce early." We trusted him, and we were beyond excited that she would come early and we would both be able to have that precious bonding time together as a family. My anxiety over my husband potentially not being there melted away, and all seemed perfect in my world.

Around that time in my life, I had started to become a very regimented person. I had been an extremely messy, unorganized child and teenager and drove my mother crazy. I never thought I would be a prepared, organized, plan-ahead type mom, but I was. I remember getting ready to go to the hospital, thinking how fabulous it was to go in with a fresh blowout, a full face of makeup, a cute outfit, and a clean house. I felt good, relaxed, excited, and ready.

The doctor came in and said it was time to break my water. He did so without any warning—and prior to my epidural being put in. It may have been the worst pain I have ever felt. That was my first twinge that maybe this wasn't the best idea. Back then, it didn't even cross my mind to doubt him or even to ask any questions, for that matter. In my mind, he was the expert; he would never, ever do anything to put me or my baby at risk. But we were in it now, so I brushed that thought aside and focused on how long we had waited for this day. Since then, I have often wondered if I had allowed her to come on her own time if anything would have been different. If maybe that little bit of extra time would have changed her immune system in some way.

The epidural was finally placed, and I calmed down and felt relaxed. I rested for a while until the nurse came in and told me it was time to push. I had never done this before; I was completely numb, and I had no idea what I was doing. As time went on, it became obvious that things were not progressing the way they wanted them to. All I remember was instantly going from being completely numb to feeling everything, all within what felt like seconds. At that point, I was beyond exhausted. My pretty blowout was a sweaty mess, my perfect makeup wiped away, and I remember feeling like I had nothing else to give, all while in the most immense pain I had ever felt.

When she was finally born, it wasn't like I had imagined at all. To this day—and my little girl is about to turn eighteen—I have never felt as close to death as I did at that moment. All I wanted to do was to bask in the miracle her dad and I had created, but all I was physically able to do was lift one finger and touch her face. The nurses then took her away, and I instantly fell asleep.

When I woke up and felt a little better than death, I finally held her. That part was perfect. I had her in my arms, and that was all that mattered at that moment. We named her Ava. Her father loved that name. To this day, I think it's one of the loveliest names I've ever heard. She was beautiful, and the worst was over. She was here; we did it. It was finally time to begin our perfect life.

They came in and out, checking on her, testing her, doing all the typical things. Again, I questioned nothing. Then they took her for her hearing test. They brought her back and casually said they would test her again in a little bit. Apparently, she had failed her newborn hearing screening. I was told it had been a hard labor, so she probably had fluid in her ears, and this was extremely common. I was not fazed at all.

The doctors eventually told us her bilirubin was a bit high, but that she could go home. She already had an appointment scheduled a few days from then and they would check her again at that time. I barely paid attention, as I could not wait to put her in her adorable going-home outfit and really begin our life as a family. It was going to be so perfect. We didn't have any family visits in the hospital; they were all out of state and had planned to visit sometime in the near future to meet her. Honestly, I was happy about that. I was not someone that wanted a houseful of people during that time.

What I thought would be a full week at home with just me and my husband turned out to be mostly just me and the baby. He was getting called into the squadron for odds and ends, and as the new guy, he felt very obligated to be at their beck and call. Meanwhile, I had a horrible time nursing. Ava was not eating or sleeping, and I felt like my eyes were bleeding with exhaustion.

I took her in for her first checkup a few days later. The second the doctor looked at her, he asked me why I had not brought her in sooner. I remember his exact words: "She looks like a highlighter." I felt worried, and stupid. I had followed the directions. I set her in the sun; I woke her up often to nurse. I was a good mom. I instantly wondered why they had not told me to come back sooner to recheck her numbers. I honestly had not realized anything was wrong.

When her numbers came back, they sent us immediately to the hospital to be admitted. I spent two nights there alone with her while she lay blindfolded underneath the lights, trying to get her bilirubin back down to a normal range. I remember feeling like I should have known better, like somehow it was my fault. But they seemed so unconcerned when we were discharged.

I was depleted when we left the hospital. I had made her appointment with the audiologist to get her hearing rechecked and tried to prepare the best I could for our incoming visitors.

After finding out Ava was deaf, I started thinking a lot about her eyes. Something in my gut told me to always be careful with them. She was about four months old when I decided we should try to transfer her to her crib at nighttime. I had a routine that I had been told about by my sister, and I was excited to start implementing it: bath, nurse, then bedtime story. My sister also had a daytime routine for naps. She called it EASY—eat, activity, sleep, your time. I always took my sister's advice as the gold standard.

The bedtime story came last so she would get used to getting put to bed awake. I said her prayers and gently laid her down. I walked out of the room and shut the door. "Why didn't you turn out the lights?" her father asked. I had hoped he didn't notice that. I was so afraid that, since she couldn't hear, if I turned out the lights and it was dark and she couldn't see, then she would be scared. I'll never forget what he told me that night. He told me not to instill my fears into her. He said that I had never worried about that before and she had been deaf this whole time, and she had slept in our room in the dark just fine. He went back in, kissed her on the forehead, turned out the lights, and shut the door.

The next few months were filled with lots of doctors' appointments, getting fitted for hearing aids, and tons of research about cochlear implants. If you have ever fit a baby for hearing aids, it is not a pleasant experience. And typically, by the time they were made and delivered, it was only a matter of weeks before they were already too small and would start falling out. It was never-ending, and even worse, they didn't work. They were hard and awkward. They would squeak and fall out constantly. I hated them. I often felt like all I did all day long was put them back in after they had fallen out, over and over and over. I was immersed in this new motherhood journey, but it wasn't like anything I had pictured.

I was alone most days. The Florida sun was hot, and Ava was too young for sunscreen, I was told, so we didn't get out much except in the early morning or late evening. Our apartment was very dark, but it had a porch that was covered, so we spent a lot of time out there. I would have coffee, research as much as I could on hearing loss, and watch her swing in the sticky Florida air. I had no friends, and my husband worked a minimum of twelve hours each day. It was a very lonely time.

My neighbor who had just recently moved in had apparently been murdered when she traveled back to her hometown for a visit. I remember thinking she looked like a nice person and that maybe we would be friends. Afterwards, I spent many days watching the police come and go from her apartment. I would watch people go in and out, removing items and eventually emptying her apartment.

This is horrible to say, because it honestly was unbelievably sad to me, but it was a source of distraction for me to watch this unfold and try to figure out what may have happened. I never found out. Oddly enough, I never researched it, either, but I have often thought about her and can still picture her face. She had dark curly hair and pale skin. I remember specifically thinking when I saw her for the first time that she seemed free and happy—almost like she was starting a new life. I never got the chance to talk to her. But I won't forget her, either. Her tragedy somehow helped deflect from focusing on my own in some weird way.

We moved to Alaska when Ava was only nine months old. I had

researched and found there were good audiologists there who could map the cochlear implants that, after much research, we had decided we wanted to get for her.

I had been taking sign language classes at the local community college in Florida and felt good about being able to finally communicate with her. I found out during that class that cochlear implants were actually extremely controversial, and that many members of the deaf community were against them. I was told it was because they felt their community would no longer exist if parents started implanting their deaf babies. I believe the fear of losing their language and culture created a divide. For our family, it felt like the right decision. We always wanted her to have the option to hear and knew implanting young would be the best chance for optimal speech development. We both said if she decided to live as a deaf person when she was older, she could just take them off. She never did. To this day, she considers it a gift. Little did I know how important a gift it would be when we found out that her eyesight was deteriorating many years later from a condition called Usher syndrome, a genetic disorder that she and her sister would share.

Alaska was an exciting adventure. We would have to travel to Seattle for Ava's surgery, but all post-op care, audiology, and speech facilities and the hard-of-hearing preschool were close by.

We bought our first house online while still in Florida, preparing for our big move. I remember the day Ava and I arrived vividly. My husband, Jeff, had taken the road trip with his best childhood friend, Brad, after deciding it would benefit us financially to move ourselves. They made the long drive together, and Ava and I had planned to visit family in Michigan before flying to Alaska after they had arrived with our things.

Looking back, I'm so glad he had the opportunity to have such an adventure with his friend. I know now, especially after his death, it is something Brad cherishes greatly. I admit, I was a bit nervous at the thought of those two traveling all that way by themselves, but I can only imagine the laughs that were had and the stories that were shared along the way.

It was summertime in Alaska, and it was so beautiful. It looked just like a picture book—God's country, for sure, and more gorgeous than I had ever imagined. It was eleven p.m. by the time Ava and I arrived and still seemed like noon. I felt so alive and ready for this new part of our life.

There, God blessed us with amazing neighbors. We knew we would have built-in fast friends in the squadron, which is always comforting, but these neighbors were not military. They just lived there. They became my angels, and I knew that God had placed me there for a very specific reason. I had no idea just how important they would become. My girls still remember Miss Ulli's weekend waffles and Mr. Dennis's famous macaroni and cheese, walks with Crazy D, endless hours of play with Miss Becky, and most importantly, all the love they felt from these amazing humans.

These were the kinds of people who let your kid eat chocolate pudding in the middle of a showroom living room with white carpet, and you knew deep down, they didn't even care if it spilled. These were good people, the kind of neighbors you wish for. They are the only people from our time in the military I still talk to, to this day. When tragedies and hardships became old news and people moved on with their own lives, they didn't. They stayed.

With that being said, I don't want to take away from our squadron stepping in during hard times. Because harder times were coming— much harder times—and God placed certain people in my life who were exactly what I needed during the most painful times in my life. Still, some people are only meant to be in our lives for a season, not forever.

I would very specifically learn this lesson in just a few short years.

How people are silenced out of fear. How even if they want to stand up and scream the truth from the rooftops, they feel an invisible gag shoved so deep down their throat that it hardens their soul. They don't say a word; they can't say a word. And I forgive them. I understand.

But watching it unfold in the kitchen of my new home, as my husband was blamed for his own death, was a life-changing, eye-opening event I wasn't prepared for. Watching two men who had loved him like brothers stand there and say absolutely nothing while the words "pilot error" were read aloud was an emotional stab like none I had ever felt before. Knowing that they knew damn well what the truth was yet still stood at attention like they agreed with the verdict, in my own home, is something I will never forget. I vowed that day to never be silenced out of fear, no matter the outcome.

Stella Rose was born a little more than two years after Ava. She came two days late, on her own terms, and it was easy. I had made a friend in Alaska named Candice. It was a dream of hers to watch a live birth. She had planned to be there to watch Stella's, and surprisingly enough, I was all in. Jeff, too, was completely fine with it. I wanted to have her witness that experience. Candice was special, like really special. Unfortunately, she got stuck in a snowstorm and missed the birth, which was easy, relaxed, and wonderful, just like Stella. But that didn't prevent her instant bond with Stella Rose the moment she was able to hold her in her arms.

The girls loved her. She instilled a strong love of our country in them at a young age. They knew when "The Star-Spangled Banner" came on, their hands were to be immediately placed over their hearts and to this day, every time I hear a patriotic song I think of Candice. She also taught the girls to always look for trash outside and to help keep our earth clean. Candice was born on Earth Day and, according to her, one of the worst things you could ever do was litter.

Candice was diagnosed with breast cancer just two years later. She had called me with the news while we were on vacation in Hawaii and would have her first chemo treatment the morning of Jeff's death, just two short weeks later. She is gone now, too, but not without leaving her imprint all over every aspect of my life, and the lives of many others. "I choose to celebrate life, rather than simply survive it," she would say. She was the strongest woman I have ever met, and I miss her.

After another failed newborn screening, we had to follow up to have her rechecked. "She is profoundly deaf," said the audiologist. This time, they were talking about Stella. I was calm, relaxed, and emotionless; I was prepared for this. I had thought about this many times while pregnant with her. I had wondered if it would happen again, and it did. I was okay. The lady running her tests looked at me like I was really weird. I actually remember her saying that she had never had anyone react to this news like I had. I didn't care. I knew what to do. I also felt a weird comfort knowing the girls would share in this and be able to help each other, support each other. This was all I had known in motherhood, and I felt confident and prepared for the challenges this time around.

The surgery trip back to Seattle this time would look a little bit different. On the first trip, we had been accompanied by one of my angel neighbors. Miss Becky was Ava's very first friend. Ava had loved Miss Becky from the moment we met her when she was just nine months old. She and her husband quickly became like family to us. She stayed with Ava while Stella was born, and Stella quickly became a huge fan as well. The girls used to sign to her using the sign for "monkey." As they were beginning to learn to hear and speak, they often read lips. If you mouth the word "Becky" and "monkey" without sound, they look exactly the same. Becky thought it was endearing and sweet, and it was. She flew with us to Seattle and offered to watch Ava for us so that we could be completely present for her big day.

Back then, they only implanted one ear at a time. Stella was only nine months old when she had her first ear implanted. We would eventually head back one last time when Ava was just over three and Stella around eighteen months. This time, they would get their second cochlear implants on the same day.

We absolutely loved our surgeon. He was amazing, and we trusted him completely. I remember him coming out of Stella's first surgery and telling me it was one of the hardest he had ever done. Her auditory nerve was wrapped around her facial nerve. He'd had to pack muscle between them to prevent her face from twitching every time her auditory nerve was stimulated by the cochlear implant. He did a beautiful job. He was prepared to see the same thing on her left ear during the second surgery, and he did.

We were lucky to have my mother accompany us for this final surgery. With her help, we were able to bounce around between the girls as needed, and she made sure they were never alone. It was hard for my mom, being so far away from her own kids. It was quite a stressful day, having back-to-back surgeries for both of your babies, and having her there definitely put me at ease. I think she was happy to feel needed. We are lucky now to all live in the same city, which is nothing we ever thought would happen.

The next two years consisted of mostly therapy sessions during the day. Both girls had multiple days of speech therapy, physical therapy, water therapy, and cochlear mappings. Ava had also started preschool at the most wonderful school with the kindest teacher. She had the most beautiful long red hair I had ever seen, and Ava adored her. She had a small classroom with a few kids, all with hearing loss, and she made dropping off my firstborn easy. I knew Ava was in the best hands.

We were beyond blessed to have the most amazing team of women supporting and loving our girls. Their audiologist, teachers, speech therapists, and physical therapists were all extraordinary women. I am still in contact with some of them today.

Two of them even showed up at my house the night the news would announce their father's death to the world. They took the girls upstairs, bathed them, and read to them while my family was downstairs staring at the television like zombies. I loved them. They were absolutely wonderful in so many ways, and I will never forget their kindness and love during that time.

CHAPTER 3
GRIEF ON STAGE

It was after ten at night on a cold November evening, if I remember correctly. I was up watching television, waiting for his call. He always called on his way home. It's funny, because I had never worried about him flying. I was so confident in his flying skills. I knew he would be able to handle any problem that might occur in whatever jet he was flying; it was just an extension of him. He loved flying, and it came extremely natural to him. I had never thought, however, about the jet failing him.

Looking back, I was very naive. I used to worry a lot about him hitting a moose on the way home from work. He was still driving my shitty two-door Cavalier from college, which was small and low to the ground. I had gotten the new fancy Tahoe, and he drove that light-blue piece of crap. It never bothered him at all, though. I used to worry he would hit the legs of the moose and its huge body would fall through the windshield onto him. It's odd, looking back now and considering what his job entailed, that I was most worried about that.

They were night flying that week, and I had quickly learned as a military wife that there was never a set start or end time to those days. I had learned early on to stick to my schedule and not work it around his. It may have seemed selfish to some, but I planned my days and schedule almost like I was a single mom. I think it had to be like that to have any normalcy. We were happy when he was able to be there, and he always just adapted.

The years he was gone a lot were sometimes a tougher transition. Things can change quickly when you have little ones. I would always have to brief him on the new rules, new disciplinary tactics, and new likes and dislikes. This is typical of a military family, I think. Reflecting on that now, I believe it prepared me for my life ahead as a widow with two small children.

Finally, my phone rang. I had thankfully already put the girls to bed and was in bed myself, mindlessly watching television and waiting for his call. Only it wasn't Jeff, like I'd been expecting—it was his squadron commander. "I'm on my way over to your house," he said. I don't remember if he said anything after that, but I knew that was bad.

I immediately called my best friend from the squadron after hanging up with him. The second I told her what he said, her only response was, "I'm on my way." I later remember her telling me that while she was on the phone with me, her husband, a fellow fighter pilot, was awakened and roused out of bed by a phone call. She said she saw him get up, throw on his flight suit, and run out the door without a word. She knew this was not normal. Something was wrong, very wrong.

When I answered the door, the commander had his wife with him and another person that, for the life of me, I cannot remember. I instantly knew what was happening before the first word was said. It's like the movies, when they knock on the door of a soldier's wife and stand there in uniform. This was the knock of death, the knock of tragedy, the last thing you hear before your world is forever changed. The only thing that made it different from the movies was that I knew they were coming.

"We can't find Jeff," he said. I remember feeling lightheaded and sitting down on the cold tiles in our entryway. I remember the tears, feeling my heart pounding, and my hand coming up to cover my mouth.

I'm not sure how long their visit lasted. It felt like I was watching it happen from somewhere else, like I was floating above near the ceiling watching myself receive this news. It was like watching myself as an actress playing a role in a movie—I can't describe it. I also remember a distinct feeling coming over me very shortly after my initial reaction. Something strange I can't put into words adequately. It felt intense and numb, strong and weak, vulnerable and angry. I stood up, and the tears stopped. They just stopped. My mind started racing. How can he be lost? How can a fighter jet go missing? Don't they have radar? Don't they have a beacon that goes off if the pilot ejects? My head was spinning. I can't remember if I asked these questions out loud or if I just thought them in my head.

Regardless, soon I would start asking questions out loud—and people didn't like that. I remember feeling numb, yet instantly I had an overwhelming feeling that something wasn't adding up. As word spread, the squadron wives started showing up. I was grateful for them. They sat with me in our living room, all of them wide-eyed and scared, yet I'm sure silently relieved it wasn't their husband. It was the thing we all knew could happen, and unfortunately some of them had witnessed scenes just like this before. One woman asked if she could pray out loud. Looking back now, it was the best thing anyone could have done.

It was November 16 in Alaska and absolutely freezing outside. I texted him, thinking maybe he had ejected and the beacon simply never went off. I didn't think to call; I never, ever called him at work unless it was an emergency. I guess internally, I believed me texting instead of calling meant he would be okay. I thought of him hurt, in the snow, trying to build a survival shelter until someone found him. Candice called that morning trying to sound hopeful. "It's been twelve hours," I said. Despite her optimism, she knew the outcome would not be good.

At this point, I had only called my sister, Kelly. She was the one who told me it was time to call his parents and sister. I didn't want to. I was stalling, hoping for a miracle. We still had no information; he was just missing. Missing in a jet that cost millions of dollars in the mountains of Alaska. That was the worst phone call I had ever had to make. I called his father first. I asked him to please drive to Jeff's sister's and mother's workplace to tell them in person. I couldn't bear the thought of them finding out over the phone.

The price tag has stuck in my head, as I recall the first page of the accident report stating that he had caused damage in the amount of $147,672,000.00 for the total destruction of the aircraft along with its internal stores. The money always seemed to be mentioned first, like it was more important than he was.

This is another lesson I learned during that time that would ring very true in the future: At the end of the day, money is always the most important. Follow the money, and it will almost always lead somewhere corrupt. This lesson would guide me quite a few years later when I was literally watching Ava fade away before my eyes and no one would help her.

The next few days were a whirlwind, to say the least. I think death in itself is traumatic enough, but this felt so public and exposed, because it was. Family arrived. People were in and out of the house from sunrise to sunset. Papers needed to be signed, decisions needed to be made. And all of this was happening while it felt like all eyes were on me.

All of those eyes on me meant that I didn't actually have time to sit in silence with my grief. I had a house full of people and two young daughters I needed to sit down and try to find the words to explain why Daddy wasn't coming back, ever. I tried my best to put myself on the backburner while I cared for so many others. Everyone else got to show up and be one with their loss; I didn't have that luxury. It didn't make it easier on anyone, but looking back, I wish I had been able to stop for a minute to process. But maybe God made it that way on purpose because he knew I needed to be on autopilot.

Thank God for the people who stepped in and actually checked things off my to-do list. I will never be able to adequately thank them. I had funeral clothes picked out and purchased for me and the girls and brought to me, something that had never entered my mind. Becky did that. She and her husband actually hosted my parents and Jeff's mother in their home. That is something only a true and selfless friend would do. The wives in the squadron at that time could have run the world. My God, were those women not only smart, but incredibly beautiful. They sure knew how to get shit done. They knew the ways of the military world in a way my family and civilian friends never could. They were savvy and used their talents to help me with business affairs and local things that needed to be checked off my list. I will never forget how incredibly amazing they were to me and the girls during that time of unimaginable loss.

Kelly was the first of my family to arrive. It was November, and she was due in early January with her third baby. She should have never been flying at that time in her pregnancy, but she pulled on her support hose, left my two small nephews at home, and made the selfless choice to make the long flight to come and be with me. She knew that I needed her. I felt such relief when she walked in the door. It was late, and I had taken an Ambien. I hugged her and fell asleep on her shoulder.

Kelly eventually called her husband, Mike, and asked him to join her, and he did. Looking back now, she was likely overwhelmed, but she never showed it. She had always been one to be ok with being on the backburner and not requiring the spotlight. The spotlight had always been carved out for me, I suppose, ever since I was a kid. She had paved my way in life and never got the credit for it. Unbelievable things that were way out of the ordinary always seemed to happen to me and she was always on standby, ready to jump in whenever needed. If I could describe her in two words, it would be indisputably reliable.

My brother-in-law soon arrived, and he went with me to meetings and guided me on documents I was signing. Mike has always been great at that sort of thing. He used his talents to help me make sound choices during a horrific time. I was unbelievably grateful.

By this time, we had finally gotten word that the ejection seat had not been activated and that Jeff had indeed gone down with the plane. The aircraft had impacted the ground in a left bank at approximately 48 degrees at a speed greater than Mach 1.1, which is over 800 mph. I was told debris had scattered up to a mile radius from the deep crater in the middle of Denali National Park where his jet plummeted into the ground. They had found papers that they knew were on his body that confirmed the dreadful news.

Over the course of the next few months, they found pieces of his flight suit and his Velcro name patch that had been perfectly sliced in half and still smelled of jet fuel when I received it months later. Recovery took nearly eight months, as the weather and location made it damn near impossible and extremely dangerous. After months of recovery with God knows how many people searching for pieces and parts of the plane, and him, a miracle happened—someone found his wedding ring. When I was called and notified, I was speechless. It was something I had wished for but never truly thought was possible. The ring had been bent into an oval. I couldn't believe it, but I could still read the inscription on the inside. To have it in my hand again brought me a sense of peace I hadn't felt since that day.

I had to chuckle to myself seeing the bent titanium ring. I remembered when we picked it out, the guy working at the jewelry store had told us at least five times that titanium would never bend or break, no matter what. I imagined Jeff standing there telling me to return it and tell him he was a liar, because it can definitely bend. Not that I didn't already know, but looking at the so-called "indestructible" titanium band, it hit me just how hard of an impact it must have been. I knew that there probably wasn't much, if any, of him left. To this day, I consider Denali National Park to be his final resting place. And I can't imagine a more beautiful spot.

I was told a few men would be coming by to interview me as part of the accident investigation. At the time, I felt married to the military and still didn't realize that I had not personally sworn in under oath. In my mind, I was still obligated to perform like a proper officer's wife. I didn't yet realize that I had a voice that I was free to use, and that I actually owed them nothing. I was still under the impression that the military cared about us, about him. We had lived in the supportive bubble of squadron life where that was true. But in the real world, up the chain of command, it was far different than I had believed. In that moment, I just did as I was told. I felt required to do everything they asked of me, and I did, without question. I had no reason to think I would ever be manipulated or misguided. I was very wrong.

After receiving the actual reports and interviews that other military members gave many months later, I noticed that they had all been asked questions prior. They were all told that anything they said could be public knowledge. They were made aware that their answers to the questions would be used in the accident investigation. They were asked if they agreed and understood, and they were also asked if there was anything they would like to say "off-the-record." I was never asked any of these things.

The day I knew they were coming, my mother was there and had planned to watch the girls and keep them occupied. I remember feeling so tired. I wasn't looking forward to doing this interview. I didn't feel like talking to more people that I didn't know. I had gotten dressed, taken a strong Valium to relax, and laid down in my bed. When they got there, I must have told someone that I wasn't able to get up to properly greet them. I remember them showing up in the doorway of my bedroom. I did allow them in, but the real question is, should they have entered?

I was interviewed in my bedroom while lying in my bed, drugged up on Valium. They were extremely good at their job. They had me fooled that they actually cared about Jeff and what kind of person he was. They wanted to know what he did for fun, what he liked on his sandwiches, what made him happy. They made me believe they were actually interested in what kind of a husband and father he was. These were all real questions they asked me. They said that they just really wanted to leave the interview feeling like they knew him.

I obliged because at that moment, it felt good to talk about him. I will always be a bit ashamed at how naive I was at thirty-one years old. As I later read back my words, I felt so violated. I sounded incredibly stupid and didn't make a lot of sense at times. They had to have known I was not right—I was stumbling over words, with countless "ums," "likes," and pauses. I don't think they cared, and I've often thought maybe they preferred it that way. I am convinced they were there for one reason and one reason only: to try to get me to say something that would help them blame the crash on him.

A dead pilot can't defend himself. And God forbid the accident could have actually been caused by something that was not his fault! I think we can all agree that this would reflect extremely poorly on our military, the government, and the contractors that make a pretty penny off of building these supersonic machines that people swoon over. I would later discover that many pilots were set up in a simulator that had recreated Jeff's exact scenario the night he died. The only difference would be that they were not actually flying for real, and they knew ahead of time what to expect. Not a single one of them survived.

The interviewers seemed overly concerned with things in our home that could have distracted Jeff, made him sick, or prevented him from getting proper sleep. I distinctly remember them being intently interested in a story I had told them about Ava waking up a few nights prior, upset that her sponge curlers had fallen out in the night, and had woken us up extremely upset about it. Like perhaps her absence of curls and her five-year-old tantrum had contributed to something so massively detrimental.

I was never told that anyone who wanted to read this interview could just look it up. That my grief-stricken, exhausted, overwhelmed, not-of-sound-mind words about personal and private things would be available for the world to see with just a search on the Internet. I was never told that his family would be able to request these documents, and my words, and that they would be sent to them without my consent. I was completely blindsided, taken advantage of in the bed that I had shared with a man I loved who had just died, all while on a drug that made me feel slow, and high, and heavy. I know that these men were just following orders, doing their job, providing for their families, but I wonder if they ever think about how wrong they were in the way they carried out their task that day.

My sister witnessed all of this unfold as she laid next to me in my bed. She still gets upset to this day thinking about that time, and she wishes she had known to protect me from the wolves in sheep's clothing. We have talked about this event many times since, and we both wish we could go back in time with the knowledge we have today and tell them to get the fuck out of my house. I vowed to never blindly comply with anything from that day forward. I am no longer afraid to go against the norm. That, I suppose, is the silver lining to the manipulative emotional assault that happened that day—I will never make a mistake like that again.

CHAPTER 4
OUR NEW LIFE

had a sense of urgency to move, to get out of that house. I knew if it were up to me, I never would have packed his things. His clothes would have remained in the closet, his toothbrush on the bathroom sink, his razor in the shower. They all would have stayed right where he left them. I needed to leave to rid myself of the daunting task of packing up his life by myself. I needed someone to come and pack it all away for me, because I knew that I couldn't.

I thought about leaving immediately but quickly realized that wasn't an option. The holidays were right around the corner. I needed to sell the house, and I needed to get through Thanksgiving and Christmas and try to squeeze out something that resembled holiday magic for the girls. My mom stayed with me for a while during this time. She helped with the girls, allowed me to go out and get drunk with my friends, and did her best to support me the best she could.

I put my sister on the hunt for a house in her neighborhood four thousand miles away. I had decided I wanted to live by her and be within walking distance of her home—those were my only two requirements. That, and I wanted a home for the girls to walk into the day we arrived. I couldn't fathom staying with someone else; I needed to give them a space that belonged to them from day one. They had been through the unimaginable, and I wanted them to have a sense of home immediately.

Kelly came through, like she always does, and found me a house a half a mile from her. I bought it over the phone, and she and my parents got the keys for me after closing. It obviously wasn't quite that simple, and there were many hands at play to make this happen. Even my realtor, who shed tears on the phone for me during the process, went well above her typical duties during this time and also became my friend. God was piecing together his disciples to make this all happen for us. My family had it cleaned and painted, bought mattresses, and stocked the fridge, all before we arrived, and my sister did all this while breastfeeding a newborn and taking care of two young boys. God, she is a saint.

While getting information on selling the house in Alaska, I discovered that we had never actually put my name on it. With the chaos of all of Ava's medical appointments, being first-time parents, and planning a huge move, that part had gotten overlooked. I panicked at first, but then I learned that I didn't have to sell it if I didn't want to; I could just walk out. This seemed so wrong and odd to me, yet the thought of having an open house and having to deal with more people made me want to curl into a ball and hide. I even called the bank to ask if this was true and what I should do. They casually told me to just leave the key and close the door, and that's what I did. I was essentially giving the house back to the bank. I'd make no profit off of it, but it wouldn't harm my credit since my name wasn't on the mortgage. I left that same day without even taking everything, the remnants of our life still scattered about that house. Closing the door to our home on that day was officially the day we said goodbye to Jeff, to Alaska, and to the last place we ever were as a family.

I was now a real single mom, a widow. God, I hated that word. And my sweet girls, to lose their dad so young—, it was a void I could never fill but vowed to dedicate my life to trying. I felt so alone traveling that day. I wondered if people at the airport could tell we were leaving behind our old life and starting a new one with just the three of us. I always felt like strangers could just look at me and tell.

I've always been very honest with the girls. The greatest advice I have ever been given in parenting was from their therapist in Alaska. She did play therapy with the girls and I used to be concerned when all of a sudden, all of their Barbies and dolls would be dead. She assured me this was very normal and age appropriate; it was their way of processing and healing.

She had thousands of toys in her office. She would take the girls in individually and then together. Out of every toy in her office, somehow the girls both picked the exact same one to represent their father. It was a white-winged Pegasus horse. Their therapist gifted it to them before we moved, and Ava still has it tucked safely in a drawer in her bedroom. Her advice was simple: She told me if they were old enough to ask the question, they were old enough for the truth. She told me when it came to the hard things to wait until they asked, then be completely honest, no matter what the question was. This advice has served me well over the years.

Walking into our new home thousands of miles away was surreal. I had only seen pictures and a few videos my sister had taken. Miss Becky had picked out the perfect paint colors for the girls' rooms, a beautiful blue for Ava and a light lavender for Stella. My sister had hired a painter to have it finished before we arrived. They were thrilled with their new special spaces, and it was heartwarming to see them smile. The house had zero furniture in it. It was huge, and it echoed with emptiness. Our things were on a barge coming from Alaska and would not arrive for a few weeks, but the girls actually loved it. It was like a huge empty playhouse for them to run free in. It was nice to hear their giggles echo as their tiny feet pounded through the empty building that we would eventually make into a home.

I couldn't believe I had bought a house I didn't plan on ever moving from. I was coming from a life where it was expected that three years was the max you would ever stay in one spot. While I was relieved that the girls seemed to love it, I remember wishing that I did, too. It felt like The Truman Show to me. All the houses looked the same, and I was reminded right away that civilian life was completely the opposite of what I was used to. People were interested, neighbors were curious. My life was an accident you couldn't look away from, and I always felt like I was being watched.

I was in insane shape when we arrived in Avon, Ohio. I had never been what you would call "overweight," but I come from a family of thick, stocky eaters, if you know what I mean. I didn't even like wearing shorts. I had been working out for about eighteen months prior to Jeff's death, but my love of carbs and treats prevented it from showing. My taste buds and cravings changed the day he died, though, and my hard-core workouts were my only release in the months that followed.

That allowed for thirty pounds of fat to fall off, revealing an extremely toned body underneath. I even had those pelvic V muscles that the singer P!nk has! I looked in the mirror and didn't recognize myself. I hadn't known that my body was capable of looking like that. In one way, I loved it; I felt strong and confident. I could go into my closet and put on anything I wanted and it looked amazing. I actually had to buy a lot of new things because I didn't have anything small enough to fit this new person that I had become.

That is when I found retail therapy. I pushed the limits of my comfort zone and wore things I would have never felt comfortable in before because, for the first time ever, I didn't give a shit what anyone thought. That felt really empowering. In a time where everything was falling apart on the inside, my outside was the best it had ever looked. I think that confused a lot of people. Weren't widows supposed to look haggard and sad? If they looked put together and happy on the outside, they must be the worst widow ever, right? Doesn't that mean they must not have loved their husband? Truth be told, I liked to keep my pain private.

I was tired of being looked at. I was tired of being expected to cry in front of everyone. I was tired of being on display. I just wanted to be left alone. I wanted to focus on my girls and give them the best life possible without people judging my every move. My life was being picked apart under a magnifying glass, and I hated it. I loved the way I looked, but I didn't love the extra judgment and meanness that I endured because of it. If you experience a tragedy and you're overweight and crying in public, people feel sorry for you. If you're rocking an amazing body and using retail and fashion to drown your sorrows while blowing off steam, people start talking.

If I told all the stories of women who all of a sudden didn't want me around their husbands anymore, you wouldn't even believe it. This included some wives from the squadron—women I was close with. That part didn't feel good at all. This is when I started learning about a thing called secondary losses, the things that come as a result of the death that you never thought about. No one ever talks about this, but it is actually a thing, and it can hurt.

Over the course of the next year, we had to get through all the "firsts" without Jeff here. We started a few new traditions and kept a lot of our old ones. I tried hard not to live in the past while making sure their father would always remain a part of their future. Parenting seemed different now. They were fragile, yet so strong, and navigating their loss while also dealing with mine seemed heavy.

I hope they know that I always tried so hard to be what they needed. Every time things started to feel more normal, something would inevitably happen to move us a few steps backwards. That first year consisted of lots of media attention, military visitors discussing the Accident

Investigation Board report, a second memorial, and the ashes of the small parts of him they did eventually find finally arriving home.

The first service was held in Alaska not even a week after his death. With it being so far from home, not many family members were able to be there. The second was at his alma mater, Western Michigan University. The love his old flight team coach and his wife showed us during that time was unbelievable. They worked tirelessly to make everything so special. The priest that had married us and baptized the girls even came to do the service. Jeff wasn't Catholic, and the service was in an airplane hangar—I'm pretty sure it probably went against the rules of the church—but he never hesitated for a second when I asked him to do it. He told me it would be his honor.

I will never forget the moment my girls were handed a flag in that hangar. Ava and Stella were in matching yellow and white dresses. Ava wore my aviator shades while Stella stood next to her, looking up at the folded flag and the man handing it to her. If you look closely at the photo, which was captured beautifully by a college friend of ours, you can see Snuggie in the crook of her tiny toddler arm.

Snuggie is Stella's blankie, her lovey. He was a twin, as the original Snuggie was lost at an airport years ago. In an attempt to console her, Jeff stopped at the nearest store and purchased two identical Snuggies, which were both immediately rejected. Slowly and reluctantly, she started to form an attachment to just one of them. Even though they were exactly the same, she somehow knew the difference. If Snuggie was in the wash and we handed her the backup, she immediately looked at us like we were idiots and refused it.

Slowly, over time, they started looking very different. Snuggie became worn, tattered, stained, and very loved. He went everywhere with her—it was a struggle to even get him in the wash. Yes, Snuggie is a boy. I can't tell you how many hours of my life have been spent looking for him. I often questioned our parenting choice of allowing her to take him everywhere we went.

Eventually, Snuggie stopped going places with us and stopped being dragged all over the house. He instead became a permanent resident of her bed. She slowly didn't need the comfort of him every minute of every day, but I'm confident if I went to check on her in the night, he would still be there to this day at almost sixteen years old.

That day at the memorial, he was there, comforting her during a moment that held such finality. Even though she was so small, just over three years old, the look on her face told me she knew something that would permanently change her life was happening.

"On behalf of the president of the United States, the United States Air Force, and a grateful nation, please accept this flag as a symbol of our appreciation for your father's honorable and faithful service."

I've often wondered about the man who spoke the words to those two small girls that day. I wonder how many times he has handed a folded flag to a child. I could not have done his job that day. But I will never forget the kindness and respect in his voice as he bent down to speak such life-changing words.

CHAPTER 5

MY FIRST DATE, MY CHAPTER TWO

The morning I saw him for the first time, I ran seven miles. I never set out to run more than one mile; I never wanted to fail. I never thought I could run more than one, honestly, even though I'd done it so many times. I'd get to one and push to two—that seemed to be the hardest part—then I'd tell myself, "I might as well try for three." Usually by that point, I'd start to feel really good and could push to five miles. It was a mental game for me.

I'd taken up running after Jeff died and began preparing for a race that my sweet friend we called Crazy Judy was planning in honor of him. I started training because I knew the race would draw in a ton of people and I didn't want to embarrass myself by not being able to finish. The race would be in the hot Texas heat, and I felt obligated to run the furthest distance, so I signed up for the 10K. It couldn't possibly have been harder than what my family was currently going through, I reasoned. In my mind, if I signed up for anything less than the longest race, it would make me seem weak or less than somehow.

I never realized how important running would be for my mental state. I had pushed myself physically that hard before as a college athlete, but the mental drive had never been there in combination with it.

That significant day, I ran seven miles. I had grown to love the runner's high. I have Judy to thank for helping me through that time in a healthy way. God knows how I would have coped if I had not felt the pressure of that upcoming race! When it was just me and my music, I felt—for the first time in my life—that exercise seemed like an escape rather than just something I had to do to look good. That is the first time I really started looking at food and movement as medicine, a life-changing awakening that would help guide me in the care of my children and loved ones for the rest of my life.

I typically ran indoors on my treadmill after the girls went to bed. Occasionally, my sister would watch the girls, and I would have the opportunity to run outside. That was my favorite. I felt free and strong. That day, I remember looking at the time and forcing myself to stop running. I had a list of things that seemed daunting and heavy to prepare for that night, although looking back now, there really wasn't a way to prepare for what I was about to do. I could have run forever that day.

It was the day Jeff's ashes were finally being flown home to me. I had waited a very long time. With the complications involved in the recovery, it was coming up on a full year since his death. It was also Ava's first day of kindergarten. God decided that handing me three extremely significant events in one day would serve me well someday, I suppose. I was sending my firstborn off without me, meeting the man that would open my heart to love again, and being given the few remains that were found of my husband all on the same day.

My purple running shorts and tank top were soaked with sweat, and I was also starving. I decided I would take Stella to Five Guys and treat myself to a burger and fries. My sister was at the photography studio next door getting baby pictures done of my sweet nephew Joseph Jeffrey and I figured they could join us.

My other nephews both have the middle name Michael, but his is

Jeffrey, named after his uncle. There are a few special souls out there named after him. Even though Joseph Jeffrey had been in utero, he was still physically with us during that hard time. I had worried about his last few weeks so much and prayed the stress I had put on my sister wouldn't negatively affect him. Thankfully, it didn't, and he was the picture of health and cuteness.

I got myself a double cheeseburger with bacon and a large fry and went to town. The four of us were sitting down at a table when two men walked in. My sister commented almost immediately that a really handsome guy was coming through the door. Two handsome men, actually, but she was referring to the younger one. The other man, I would learn in due time, was his uncle. He was also extremely handsome, and I would eventually grow to learn so much from him and consider him a mentor in my life.

I looked up mid-bite and made brief eye contact with him, my hair, still wet from sweat, covered in a brown train conductor's hat. The mystery man had thick hair dark that curled up around the bottom of his baseball hat. He was tall and muscular with full lips and wore one of those three-quarter-sleeve baseball T-shirts.

"Yeah, he is cute," I said—and that's all it took to get her wheels turning. It was getting to be that time in my journey, almost a year after Jeff's death, when people were starting to ask if I wanted to date again. Some of these people, I didn't even know. People seemed overly interested in that area of my life for some reason. Some squadron friends wanted me to find another military man, to rejoin the life I had been living prior. I admit, I had thought about that. I simply couldn't imagine living any other life, and it scared me to live what I considered a "normal" one.

However, I wasn't really interested in getting back out into the dating world, to be honest. And if I ever did, I knew I would have so many stipulations on the list in my head. I didn't think many men who fit my qualifications would even give my situation the time of day. A widow with two deaf daughters probably wasn't on the top of anyone's list, and the thought of navigating a relationship amongst all the other things I was doing honestly seemed like a chore. I wasn't supposed to be dating at this phase in my life, and I really didn't want to be. My sister, once again, knew better.

My focus was solely on the girls. I was one hundred percent involved in every aspect of their lives. They were my whole world now, and for the first time, I wasn't confident in my parenting. There was no handbook on how to do this; I was constantly second-guessing all of my parenting choices and desperately trying to fill a void in their lives that could never be filled. It was an endless struggle, yet I was fiercely protective and adamant about doing it all.

Still, I did have quite a few visitors that first year. But even when I did let loose and go out, I didn't leave the girls with a babysitter until they were completely ready for bed. Thankfully, over time I found a few amazing babysitters I trusted, and that part slowly got easier. Little by little, I allowed myself more freedom. Kelly sister was my only friend there for a long time. I didn't really do anything other than exercise, be a mom, and hang out with her. I think she wanted me to feel like a woman again, even for a moment. To get dressed up for a night, and to have an adult conversation. To escape my reality for a few hours. I didn't realize that I needed that, but she did.

As we walked out of Five Guys that day, the two men were sitting at a table just outside the door. We decided to grab ice cream around the corner and come back to sit outside and indulge before leaving, and I remember my sister telling me to go talk to him. I actually laughed out loud. "Oh, sure, I'll tell him I'd love to go out sometime, but I can't tonight because my dead husband's ashes are coming home. That would be the best pickup line ever," I said while rolling my eyes.

I stood up, knowing my back was to him, and looked up at my sister with a sly smile and purposely dropped my keys on the ground. "Whoops, I dropped my keys," I said to her, bending over very slowly to pick them up, knowing full well my amazingly toned ass was on full display with my barely there running shorts, just a few feet away from this handsome stranger's gaze. It was a time in my life where I did random things just for the reaction alone. I was always joking around and trying to find ways to make light of heavy situations. I knew that would make her laugh, and it did.

I then told Kelly I was leaving and Stella and I walked to the car. As I was pulling up to the light to turn left out of the complex, though, I saw her. Kelly had pulled her van up in front of their truck. What in the actual hell is she doing? I thought to myself. I saw her get out and run up to their door. The light turned green, and I was forced to turn and stop watching whatever it was she was doing unfold.

My phone rang a few short minutes later. "He's single, he's a fireman, he definitely noticed you, thinks you're cute, and wants to take you out. I have his number for you," she rambled excitedly. I asked if he had asked for my number, to which she quickly replied, "Absolutely not!" Kelly can be a bit forward with her matchmaking, but she's not stupid. My sister is known for her matchmaking skills. She thoroughly enjoys this type of thing, so her behavior on this day was not a surprise to me. I immediately told her I was hanging up the phone!

She later brought over a ripped piece of a greasy Five Guys fry bag with the name Nick and a phone number on it. I do remember noting that it might have been the nicest penmanship I had ever seen from a man. I put it on top of my growing pile of mail that went unanswered in a silver bowl on my counter.

I then went to my closet to pull out the outfit I would wear to the airport to pick up the wooden box filled with the only remains of my husband that had been found. The dress I had picked out was periwinkle blue, and it was very plain. It was short, but not too short, and sleeveless. I wore my favorite white-and-nude Cole Haan sandals, my hair was down and straight in a short blonde bob, and my makeup was subtle. I looked like the perfect widow.

I masked my nerves that day for the girls. I had gotten very good at that. Hiding emotions and protecting them from facts that were far too grown-up for their wounded little hearts had become a part of my daily life. They had no idea what I was going to do that day. Again, I was following the words of wisdom from their therapist in Alaska. They had not asked, and I was grateful I didn't have to explain.

After that, a few weeks went by, and I honestly think my sister was getting tired of being my only source of entertainment. She told me that I was going to text the fireman and go out for a drink. It didn't have to mean anything—it was just a chance to take off the mom hat for a moment and get out of the house. So, I did.

We had planned to meet at a little wine bar not far from my house. I wore a short little white lace shift dress from Ann Taylor Loft, and I felt really pretty. In fact, I felt a little guilty that I was kind of excited. I don't know if I was excited about the date or just excited to have a reason to get dressed up that didn't involve anything sad. He called me on my way there so we could figure out where to meet up. I had never heard his voice before, as we had only texted just a few times, and it completely took me by surprise. His voice was the deepest, most masculine voice I had ever heard in my life.

I wasn't even sure he would recognize me, seeing as the day he first saw me, I had been unshowered, sweaty, and stuffing a double bacon with cheese in my mouth. Plus, the little stunt I had pulled to make my sister laugh didn't allow him much time to look at my face! But somehow, he did. He caught a glimpse of my face outside the wine bar and smiled, well before he even had a chance of recognizing me by my lower half. We gave each other the semi-awkward "nice to meet you" hug, and he was bigger than I remembered. He was tall, broad, and muscular. I remember his back feeling like a brick wall when I patted it during our introduction. He was also extremely handsome with really good hair.

I quickly realized I had forgotten how to do this. The last time I was on a date, I had been a teenager! I was now a full-grown woman with a past, and more importantly, I was also a mother. I had not really thought it through that I didn't want this stranger to know any details about me, especially that I was a mom.

My story had garnered so much media attention, and I was so protective of the girls. My mind started racing, wondering if he was a serial killer or a kidnapper. I deflected questions the whole night. I talked about my childhood and college life. We discovered we had one thing in common—we had both been college athletes. I was on the synchronized skating team, and he was a baseball player. We talked a lot about that.

I asked him a ton of questions and gave vague responses when he asked me anything about my current life. I did anything and everything I could think of to not talk about my actual current reality. Eventually, I was forced to tell him I had moved from Alaska after he asked about my bright-yellow license plates that I had not prioritized changing yet. He had seen them that day at Five Guys, and I would later discover that he originally thought they were "party plates." In the state of Ohio, drivers who have received restricted driving privileges after a DUI must display yellow license plates, which just so happened to be the same color yellow as my Alaska plates.

We had a nice time, and the conversation, despite my deflections, seemed to flow. He was very much a gentleman. I wrapped it up early to keep it short and sweet so I could get back to my girls. I didn't like leaving them, but it did feel really good to get out.

Little did I know that my secretive nature would eventually lead him to believe that I might be married and looking to cheat on my husband. The day he found out the truth, he'd had a whole speech prepared. He was ready to tell me what a horrible person I was and kick me to the curb! To say I rocked his world with the truth would be an understatement.

It was a surreal feeling driving home that night. That date really reminded me, like a punch in the gut, that I was living a completely new and foreign life. But at the same time, it also felt okay for me to be open to new possibilities, and to allow myself to have a little fun. I remember feeling that maybe, eventually, it would be okay for me to open my heart again. Maybe one day, I could still be a good mom and also allow myself to love again. But it would take some time for me to make peace with that.

And eventually, God would give me permission to do just that. He would tell me that my heart was meant to love again. He would tell me that I had fulfilled my marital commitment to Jeff till death do us part. He would allow me not to feel guilty and remind me that I deserved a life with someone to love me, too. That I was allowed more than just to be a caretaker for my girls. That it was okay for me to begin to heal, too. He would allow me to have a future, to have another wonderful, supportive family to love me and my girls. Another group of strangers that would one day turn into family, willing to accept me and my daughters without judgment and treat them as their own. And not only did my heart love again—it burst wide open a few years later when we welcomed our son, Vincent, into the world.

I had never thought I would have any more children, let alone a boy. After having the girls, I could not have imagined anything but that, but Vinny turned out to be everything I never knew I needed. A missing piece I never knew was lost. I could not imagine life without him. Holding him in my arms was the true meaning of life after death to me.

He made everything make sense in the world, in a weird way that I can't begin to try to explain. He is truly one of my life's greatest blessings, and I am so lucky that I get to be his mom.

That was the first time in years I felt like God knew what he was doing. Vinny is special in a way that is difficult to describe in words. He has filled the holes in my heart since day one. He is funny and sweet, smart and athletic. He is obsessed with the outdoors and all the creatures of the world, big and small. He is fiercely protective of me and his sisters and has always been fully aware of his role and duty to defend and keep us safe, even at his young age. I pray daily for his future spouse, as well as for the girls and their future spouses. He will be a phenomenal husband and father someday, and whoever he marries will be the luckiest girl in the world. Growing up in our family has given him the kind of empathy you can only get from witnessing struggle. He is now nine years old and loves his family with all his heart, and his sisters absolutely adore him.

CHAPTER 6
NEW DIAGNOSIS, NEW TRADITIONS

The official diagnosis of Usher syndrome was shocking physically to hear, but internally, I wasn't surprised. My gut had always told me there was something more going on than Ava just not being able to hear.

I remembered thinking back to the day we first put Ava to bed in her crib alone and how I had wanted to leave the lights on. Something in my gut felt unsettled that day, but I could never put a finger on it. I am still so glad that Jeff turned the lights out that night; he taught me not to instill my fears into her. But deep down my mother's instinct told me something else was lurking, and again, I was correct.

Usher syndrome is the most common form of combined deafness and blindness, and it is genetic. There are a few different types and sub-types. The girls both have type 1B, which is typically severe to profound hearing loss at birth coupled with severe balance issues and followed by vision loss, typically starting with night blindness in early childhood.

The girls were both very late walkers and were constantly tripping over and running into things. I always had to surround them with pillows when they were babies and learning to sit. There were times they would just fall off the chair during dinner if they turned their head too quickly. I was always the only mom at the park carrying a baby while two steps behind Ava, going up every slide right behind her. I remember one time I received a judgmental comment from another mom about how it was dangerous for me to carry my baby up steps at a bounce house. If only she had known how dangerous it actually would have been if I didn't and Ava tumbled backwards and sent a cascade of children down with her. I was used to the comments by then, but I can't say they didn't hurt sometimes.

Riding a bike was difficult, and the girls used training wheels for an extremely long time. I know many children with Usher syndrome who never master bike riding. Even now, if you see them riding a bike, they may appear a bit tipsy. Familiar places are much easier, but new places are harder, especially if it's dark out. They compensate extremely well; however, I have always reminded them of a sloping hill or uneven ground. Even to this day, I never, ever put knives facing up in the dishwasher or leave it open.

I've always enjoyed researching. I think it really started when Ava was born deaf and I had to advocate for her, and it continued throughout my life as a caregiver for the girls. As my distrust of authority grew after Jeff's death, my drive to research for myself emerged in full force. I believe it's been a blessing to have the drive to constantly dig deeper than just believing what the experts tell me. I specifically remember bringing a piece of paper with the words "Usher syndrome" on it to the doctor's office one day well before the diagnosis and asking that doctor if she thought the girls could have it. She quickly replied stating that she didn't think so; they had received a thorough eye exam prior to moving from Alaska and there were no concerns there.

I didn't automatically trust her like I had done in the past just because she was supposed to be the expert; I was learning to question things now. I was learning to follow my gut. This time, I didn't believe her. I made appointments to have their eyes tested again, this time with retinol imaging done. My instincts were correct, and again I was thrown a curveball I had already felt in my gut, but it still hit hard to know for sure. There was no cure for this. It made me feel helpless. Was I just supposed to sit around and do nothing? Just accept this horrible diagnosis and move on?

I decided I couldn't do that. I wasn't that person who just accepted something anymore. I started diving in and found that very little research had actually been done on Usher syndrome, and it seemed like money was the one thing preventing that from happening. Of course, it was no surprise to me that once again, money seemed to be the most important factor. That's when I started Sisters for Sight. It started as a simple Facebook page. It was therapeutic for me to write. I felt a little vulnerable sharing our story, but I felt it was time. It was my way of having a platform to start sharing about this horrible disease that people didn't seem to know anything about and to eventually raise funds for scientific research. I needed to at least feel proactive.

This is the part of social media that I love. The physical human connection may not be there, but the opportunity to connect with like-minded people to join forces is strong. The flip side of social media, however—the evil side—would prove to launch a series of events that almost took Ava from me in more ways than one many years later.

The power, control, and brainwashing that can be done to a child confined to their room in isolation from Covid, while not being allowed to socialize the old-fashioned way, may have been one of the most dangerous things to ever happen in our time. I couldn't just sit back and accept that this was happening to my sweet girls and do nothing about it.

As the years moved forward, we gained many followers, and people became invested in our story. We joined forces with parents who were much more tech-savvy than I was and started channeling our funds to their nonprofit called Save Sight Now. Invested, desperate, and motivated parents are a force like nothing I have ever seen. I am proud to say that since I began sharing our story, we have been able to significantly contribute toward vital research to support and advance emerging treatments. We hope to help finance future potential clinical trials to help end childhood blindness and find a cure for Usher syndrome type 1B. I have immense hope that a cure will be found in their lifetime.

This was also when my Halloween tradition started. Holidays had lost their sparkle and magic; the thought of dressing up seemed like a chore. Night vision had already become an issue with the girls, and navigating small children through the dark became a daunting and stressful task. To be honest, I dreaded it. We would leave as early as possible to try to get as much daylight and as little darkness as we possibly could, and I would strap them up with headlamps and flashlights. They would still trip, fall, knock over toddlers, and run into bushes.

They still were as joyful as any other kid on Halloween, but it killed me to watch. They didn't feel the magnitude of it like I did, and I was grateful for that. I felt jealous and angry sometimes watching all the other moms, walking together, husbands by their sides with drinks in hand, letting their little ones run free from house to house. I couldn't do that. That day specifically was always a reminder of how hard their life was.

I felt a need deep inside me to start new traditions and bring the fun back somehow. I had stopped being fun after Jeff died. I knew that I was fully responsible for every little thing now, and it overwhelmed me in a way that didn't allow for much fun. Or at least that was what I told myself that, and I believed it. I was tired, stressed, and alone.

I would leave certain tasks that typically didn't fall under my umbrella undone, as if someone might come along and just magically take care of them. Sometimes, that might be something as minor as taking the trash cans to the street on garbage day. I hated that job. I would look at them up against the house and it would make me so angry. It wasn't my job, and I wasn't supposed to be in charge of it. I eventually realized how stupid that was when our garbage didn't get picked up one day and I had no room left in the can for next week's trash, and I stopped doing that. I realize how silly that sounds, but sometimes it's the littlest, most insignificant things that make you understand the magnitude of how life changes when someone you love dies.

No one was coming to rescue me. No one else was completing what I considered to be the "manly jobs" around the house unless I specifically asked them to—and I didn't like asking. I prided myself on being able to handle it all, and I still do sometimes. That was a mistake. No one should ever feel ashamed to ask for help, but I never wanted to feel like a burden to anyone.

To this day, I tell the girls that we don't use the bad things that have happened to us as an excuse to be a shitty person or a lazy human or less that we are capable of. I've seen people do that, and I think it's sad and pathetic. I never wanted to be that person.

After realizing their vision would keep deteriorating, creating visual memories for our new life became so important to me. It was a small way for me to say yes to something I'd always said no to—maybe a way for them to see me as fun again. So, I decided I would start to dress up. It would be a surprise, and they wouldn't know ahead of time what I would dress up as. I would send them off to school and make sure I was completely transformed when they got off the bus.

I didn't realize how much the girls would look forward to the anticipation of seeing my costume each year. They had always asked me to dress up with them, and I had always said no. Sometimes I'd throw on a cowboy hat real quick as we walked out the door, but typically I would tell them I didn't have time or that I was too focused on getting them ready. It wasn't until Usher syndrome entered our lives that I thought about how easy it would be to actually say yes, and what a wonderful visual memory it could be for them to remember this tradition.

I always tried to pick something they were really into each year. When they were small, it was easy. I have been the Queen of Hearts, Maleficent, Mrs. Incredible, Poppy the Troll, and Glinda the Good Witch. As they got older, it became harder. Sometimes I would aim for something that would just make them laugh, like the year I dressed up as Karen who needed to speak with the manager. They were also slightly embarrassed of me during their tween years, like the time I met the bus fully transformed into Lady Gaga in her Super Bowl leotard.

Kelly was substitute teaching at that time at the middle school. The next morning, she overheard two teachers gossiping. They were whispering about a mother in their neighborhood trick-or-treating with her two small daughters who was dressed like a hooker. She politely asked them what this woman was wearing and they described the bedazzled black leotard, long blonde wig, fishnets, and tall studded boots. My conservative sister sweetly explained what the actual costume was and the story behind it. I am sure they instantly felt ashamed and embarrassed.

When she told me, I couldn't stop laughing. In a way, I couldn't blame them for discussing it. It had been a while since I had tried it on, and I will admit I had gained a few pounds. For my more extravagant costumes, I would begin to plan them out months prior and had actually had the outfit for some time by this point. Admittedly, it was a tad cheekier than I had planned. If this had happened to me prior to Jeff's death, I would have been extremely embarrassed and self-conscious and probably would have contemplated not wearing it at all. But that night, I just decided to own it. I knew the girls wouldn't care. I also knew people might feel the need to discuss, but I told myself I would just rock it with confidence regardless. And I did! A little extra ass had never stopped me before, and it certainly wasn't going to stop me from continuing our tradition.

I was used to people thinking they had a right to critique my decisions, to comment on my body, or to dissect my personal life, so a part of me welcomed the controversial discussions. Part of me wanted them talking and not knowing the reason behind everything. It kept them away from us. In a way, I felt protected by just being an interesting gossip session, but not someone you actually wanted to talk or hang out with. I knew by then to choose my friends wisely. I knew that a person needed prove their loyalty before I shared too much. I was a bit hardened by this point from much worse criticism in my past, when people didn't think I was "widowy" enough, so it didn't bother me. But my sister made it a point to always stick up for me, which I appreciated.

As the girls became older and too cool to trick-or-treat, it became so much easier. I wasn't dragging them out, holding their hands as they ran up a dark, uneven yard to get their candy, or apologizing to the parents who glared at us because my girls accidentally bumped into their children. I couldn't stop and explain to every single person they accidentally bumped into, so I just kept apologizing over and over. That part was hard. I did want them to know the reason for the girls' sake. I wanted empathy for my sweet girls, not the face of an angry adult who thinks your child is purposely knocking over their toddler to get to the candy first. In their teen years, they would just set up shop in the driveway with friends and a fire and pass out the candy, and I admit I had a small sense of relief when that time came.

Their age never stopped me from keeping my costume a surprise, and I still waited until they got home from school for the big reveal. This year, I even rolled into Stella's work as Barbie because she couldn't get the night off and I knew she wouldn't want to miss out! She happily welcomed me and we snapped a quick picture together and she gave me a hug. These were the years of Eleven from Stranger Things, Kim Kardashian in her pink bodysuit from Saturday Night Live, and most recently, roller Barbie. The girls absolutely love it, and surprisingly, so do their friends. I made a promise to do it until they both graduated from high school, and it saddens me that that time is almost upon us.

Changing the narrative of Halloween truly turned a day of fear and stress into a day of excitement and joy. I hope, when they look back on this tradition, they feel warmth in their heart and the unconditional love I have for them. And I also hope that no matter the vision loss, they will be able to picture all the costumes vividly in their minds and, more importantly, feel the love that went into surprising them each year.

I had never actually wanted to physically harm someone before—that is, until I met who we now refer to as "Covid Curt." Covid Curt was the manipulative, conniving vulture whose predatory actions were the start of Ava's medical downward spiral. If I see his mugshot on the news someday, I will not be surprised at all.

Covid was a weird time for everyone. It was an unprecedented time, and I think all parents made choices and allowed things that they typically wouldn't have. Ava was in her eighth-grade year and Stella in her sixth when the pandemic started. I remember that weird, uneasy feeling the day we were told to clean out their lockers and head home. It was like the whole world shut down in an instant. At first, I remember enjoying the calmness of the house. Not having a million places to run and having my whole family at home felt nice. Being forced to slow down and stick close to home was comforting in a way. Little did we all know that those two weeks would turn into years, and the damage done during that time, especially to children, would change the world as we knew it forever.

The girls were definitely not the first amongst their peers to get phones; they were probably some of the last, and social media was forbidden. We had rules and codes they needed me to enter to have screen time or play a game. They turned their phones into me at night by a certain time and knew I had access to peek whenever I wanted. I did what most parents I know do when their children hand over a device that could strip away the innocence they would do anything to protect. Covid broke many of these rules, and I often wonder if it was designed that way on purpose.

As weeks turned into months and summer came and went, it was time to start school again. As we all know, the first day back looked very different that year. The fear instilled in all of us was still there, and not many of us questioned anything at that point. Many of us were sheep. I am embarrassed to admit I was one of them. There were mandatory masks, social distancing, and some schools even split time between in-person and at-home learning, as in Ava's case. Every time a kid in their class tested positive, there was a quarantine. I don't remember a time where I didn't have a child home in their bedroom streaming into their classroom.

My children's bedrooms had turned into mini apartments. We had never allowed food in their rooms prior. As I would sneak in, trying not to disrupt class or be seen by a classmate without a bra or in my bathrobe, I collected cups, plates, bowls of food, and wrappers on a daily basis. The phones that had once been collected like clockwork now stayed with them later and later. Their need for social connection along with my guilt allowed it. Overnight, their worlds turned mostly digital, and their connections only existed behind a screen.

Eventually Instagram was allowed, but with parameters. It seemed to happen so slowly, like a lobster dropped in a pot of cold water and boiled. I hardly noticed the changes creeping in due to the magnitude of the unknown that was happening in the world. Friendships formed with people they were never even allowed to be within six feet of, friends I had never met, whose faces they had never seen.

I began learning the ways of navigating a pandemic with a teenager and a little bit about how Instagram worked. They would assure me they would never accept requests from anyone they didn't know or anyone who didn't have mutual friends. This seemed to be the new way of life. I didn't like or understand it, but I tried my best to stay with the times, I suppose.

This is when Covid Curt entered the picture. He was a student at a nearby school with a few mutual friends. I figured, naively, that it was harmless. Ava was in high school by then, and I knew that talking to boys would eventually become a regular occurrence I would have to get used to. I just remember wishing it was in a simpler time, like when I was in high school and I'd have to stretch the long phone cord from the kitchen wall to the top basement step and shut the door to have even a few minutes of privacy. A time when you actually had to talk using your voice and pick up the phone without knowing who was on the other end, though we did eventually get caller ID and call waiting. It was the coolest!

As the months passed, people started going out and about a little more, and the girls were itching to get back into the hustle and bustle of even a fraction of what life was like before. Ava and Curt had wanted to meet in person for a while by then. I had avoided it for as long as I could, but I finally agreed. She wasn't allowed to drive with him; he was two grades older and already had his license. I agreed to take her to a nearby outdoor mall that was extremely public. I wanted to meet him in person and gave them two hours to go get a hot chocolate, walk around, and get to know each other. As a mom, I really felt like I had taken all the precautions to provide her a little freedom while still having the proper parameters in place to keep her safe. I met him, shook his hand, reminded him that she was not allowed to drive with him, and even saw where his car was parked so he knew that I was aware and watching. He was extremely polite and said all the right things. My baby was fifteen and growing up, and it made me happy to see the smile and excitement on her face. Sometimes we can all be fooled by evil pretending to be innocent and pure, especially when you see it ignite a flame of joy inside someone you love who has been handed an extremely tough hand in life.

Ava would eventually share her very first kiss with this monster. I remember feeling a little panicked. So much for the social distancing, right? I was trying to give her a little bit of normalcy in a world that was upside down. How could I be mad about this? This was a normal part of experiencing life as a teen girl! I tried to remember to feel blessed that my daughter was coming to me to share this moment. I remember thinking that I must have done something right if I was one of the first people she rushed to tell.

Turned out Curt had Covid, and now unfortunately so did Ava. How many people can say they got Covid from their very first kiss? What should have been a sweet moment she would remember fondly turned into a week of isolation up in her room while I feverishly cleaned and disinfected every square inch of the house. Up and down the stairs I went multiple times per day, bringing her meals and vitamins, and I eventually gave her even more time with her phone, which unfortunately meant more time with him.

I remember feeling so guilty keeping her away from the rest of us, so in a way I was glad she had him to chat with to pass the time. Little did I know this was the start of him making plans for them, explaining to her his sick expectations, and sending explicit videos of himself doing things no parent wants to imagine their daughter watching.

Even my nephews, who were roughly the same age, were absolutely appalled after my sister explained the situation to them. And these are extremely handsome, athletic young men who have never in their life had to try very hard to get a date. They were completely disgusted and shocked, which should tell you how appalling and abnormal his requests were. They even offered to go find him and beat him up. I know this may sound crazy, but hearing that offer warmed my heart and made me love them even more. Coming from a teenage boy, it says a lot about their need to protect their cousin. I've often thought about how lucky the women they marry someday will be.

I had read a few of the text messages between Ava and Curt, unbeknownst to Ava, and I didn't appreciate the way that he worded things; it didn't sit well with me. I could tell by her short responses that she was uncomfortable with the situation as well but was unsure of how to handle it. Unfortunately, the majority of their communication must have been via FaceTime, and those horrible Instagram videos that delete automatically after they are viewed just one time. I prodded a bit as I would come to check on her. I didn't dig too much; I just started a few conversations on my views of how a man should treat a woman. I could see the wheels spinning and knew deep down it couldn't be good. I knew I had time, as her quarantine was not yet finished, but she had already spoken of their plans to see each other immediately after it ended.

Less than twenty-four hours had passed, and she asked to talk to Nick, and me. This was a bit of a red flag in itself; she typically never came and sought him out to talk. I don't even think she realized at the time, but her gut was telling her she needed protection, the kind of protection you don't get from your mom. We tried hard to just listen. When a teenager opens up, you shut your mouth for as long as you can and open your ears. As she spoke about the horrific things that had transpired and the disgusting things he was requesting from her, I had my hand on Nick's back. He was wearing a thin blue T-shirt. I could feel his breath quicken and as I lifted my hand, its mark was left behind fully intact in sweat.

The hardest part for me was when she innocently asked if that was just what all boys asked girls to do. I could have killed him right then and there and slept soundly that night. Then I looked over at Nick's face and thought to myself, Oh shit, Nick's going to seriously kill Covid Curt. I don't think I had ever seen that look on his face before.

Poor Ava left the conversation that night knowing what had transpired was wrong, but naively thinking that if she just told him those things made her uncomfortable, all would be well. I secretly allowed this scenario to play out knowing full well how angry she would be at the plan we had devised. Nick wanted to see this punk in person and talk to him face-to-face. He told Ava she was allowed to invite him over the day their quarantine ended.

I felt so horrible watching her getting ready that day, picking out her outfit, making her hair and makeup so pretty. I saw his car pull up as she was flying out the door to greet him. As I turned, I saw Nick quickly sliding into his giant hunting boots to get there first. He was doing that fast walk, not quite a run, as he brushed past me with eyes locked on his target. There was nothing stopping his six-foot-four, 250-pound frame of pure power with a look in his eyes that no teenage boy wants to see coming at him. "Ava, go in the house. I've got it from here" was all I heard from inside.

Nick had been smart and consulted with the police prior to the chat he was planning on having. Curt had lied about his age and was actually a year older than we had thought, but not quite an adult, which meant the situation needed to be handled delicately. The policeman, who was also a friend of ours, told him that hearing the story made the daddy hairs on the back of his neck stand up, and he advised Nick of exactly what he could do within the law. He also discretely told him that if Curt came at him in an aggressive manner to make sure it was on our property and not on the tree lawn, insinuating that would be the best place to give him what he deserved and all would be alright. I know Nick was secretly hoping that scenario would happen, but it didn't. But I knew with one hundred percent certainty that after he was done with him, we would never ever see Curt again.

The walls of Ava's bedroom and the safe space of our home were not enough to protect her naive, innocent self from this predator who was out for one thing. I'm sure you all expect me to say that I wish this never happened to her, which is true in some ways. But since it did, I can honestly say I am glad it happened under our roof, where she had love, guidance, and protection. I cringe to think of what could have happened otherwise. The lesson learned from the experience will forever remind her to always trust her gut and use her voice. It left emotional scars that she is still working through, I am sure, but it also provided wisdom that can only come from experience. I am forever grateful she followed her own intuition enough to know it was time to ask for help and even more grateful that she can share the awful things in life with me, not just the good ones. That in itself will always mean the most.

Something inside her changed that day as she saw his bright-yellow Camaro drive away from our house. It would take her a full six months to be able to verbalize that she understood what we did and why, even though I know deep down, she already understood the day she came to talk to us. But the fact that she knew and actually appreciated the protection and guidance didn't take away from the fact that she was still angry and hurt. Her internalized trauma was unfortunately taken out on us.

I've often heard that it takes three things to trigger your immune system to go haywire: genetics, an environmental or viral component, and something that deregulates your nervous system, like a traumatic event or injury. The perfect storm—the trifecta creating the disastrous effect inside her body—had been concocted, and none of us were prepared for what the next two years would bring.

CHAPTER 8
THE LITERAL SHIT SHOW

As a general rule, elevated levels of calprotectin in your stool indicate intestinal inflammation. This could be anything from a bacterial or parasitic infection to colorectal cancer or an inflammatory bowel disease such as ulcerative colitis or Crohn's disease. Typically, a level of 50 or less is considered normal. By the time Ava was hospitalized, her levels were well above 3,000. Her white blood cell count was high and her hemoglobin very low. She didn't even make it to the start of her GI appointment that day. After filling another toilet full of blood while waiting to be called back, she could barely walk into the exam room. As the nurse tried taking her blood pressure, she was so lethargic, she was barely responding. The squad was called and she was instead taken by ambulance next door to the main campus and admitted.

She should have been admitted the previous two nights that I had driven her into the ER with excruciating stomach pain. They even found blood in her stool, and yet they still decided to send her home with Maalox due to the fact that she had an upcoming GI appointment scheduled. I should have pushed back harder and insisted that she wasn't in any state to be sent home, and the so-called "experts" never should have allowed it. At the time I was not well versed in GI issues, as no one in my family had ever experienced that before.

I still feel guilty, as she'd had her monthly cycle that week and had complained of it being extremely heavy and painful. I think it definitely masked what was actually happening, and I wonder now if I had caught on a few days earlier than I did, if perhaps it would have prevented even a fraction of the suffering she endured. I don't think she even realized at that point where exactly the blood was coming from, and being a typical teenager, she didn't tell me that very important part. I continued to give her Motrin, which I now know is the worst thing I could have done, for what I thought was just bad menstrual cramps and sent her to school. It was the end of her freshman year and she had finals coming up; we were just trying to push through.

Those finals were never taken, and she didn't return to school that year. She spent the remainder of what was left of that school year in the hospital. Along with what we would soon find out was ulcerative colitis, she had a pretty severe C-diff infection along with it. That meant she was confined to her room, even though she didn't have the energy at that point to even want to leave. Thankfully, I was able to stay with her the entire time, swapping out here and there for a few hours with family members to run home for a shower or to collect personal things we needed. I even set up our essential oil diffuser, which was an unbelievable help. If anyone reading this has witnessed a GI bleed with a C diff infection, you can only imagine how welcoming the scent of those oils were. I do remember feeling guilty leaving the others at home, not even being able to welcome them home on their last days of school as summer vacation began. Stella was a gem during that time, as she always is, helping with Vinny and around the house.

I didn't have much else to do in the hospital besides tend to Ava, so I did what I do best: I dove headfirst into research and quickly educated myself on all things ulcerative colitis. Decisions needed to be made rather fast, considering how sick she was. I was told at that time that immuno-suppressant medications needed to be started immediately with steroids to bridge the gap, giving them time to work. I was also told that she would need to remain on these medications forever or until they stopped working.

I was informed that it's recommended to stay on them as long as possible before switching to another, as there are only a handful of options and most of them cannot be restarted after stopping because the body will produce antibodies and they will no longer be effective. Once a person has tried them all unsuccessfully, removing the colon and using a colostomy bag would eventually be the only option. This was terrifying to me. A drug called Remicade was recommended and was waiting on insurance approval. While researching, I realized this would be done as an infusion that could happen anywhere between every four to eight weeks for the rest of Ava's life. I'm not really sure how that one ended up being pushed back on the waitlist, but in the end a drug called azathioprine was recommended as the best fit for her. It was a pill that would be taken nightly and at the time seemed much easier than spending an entire day every few weeks receiving an infusion.

I agreed to most of their recommendations. I was walking Ava to the bathroom sometimes over ten times per hour, watching the toilet fill with blood. I was holding her hair back as she vomited while trying to suck down the multiple plastic cups of liquid she needed to take to prepare for her colonoscopy. She was pale and seemed so frail. I knew this was not the time to drag things out. I was told that suppressing the immune system would calm the inflammation and allow the colon to heal, but this also meant that she would be more susceptible to getting sick. If she did get sick, it would take even longer to heal or put her at risk for more serious infections. Hearing this in the middle of a pandemic made it extra frightening and nerve-wracking. I was assured that it was safe, that uncontrolled disease would be a much worse outcome than the list of possible side effects of the medications, which were all very, very long and scary.

A soft GI diet was put in the orders, and they allowed her to pick from that menu. It seemed incredibly odd to me. Grilled cheese on white bread, French toast, and Sara Lee apple pie were a few of the options that were allowed. Although I have to laugh now, because if you were to ask Ava if she remembers anything good about that hospital stay, she would still say it was those damn Sara Lee pies. I remember thinking, This is not nutrient-dense or healthy at all. I had dabbled in the holistic approach for a while by that time and always prided myself on teaching my children the importance of healthy food choices, but the doctors explained to me the importance of her eating food that her GI tract didn't need to work hard to digest.

Nick's ears must have been ringing at how this food disgusted me, because at this time he was at home preparing a huge pot of organic homemade bone broth that he would eventually deliver to her in large thermoses. That, along with the iron-filled steak and crab his sister delivered, made me feel somehow better than watching Ava shovel down that hospital food filled with God knows what. The doctors didn't seem overly concerned at all with how diet would impact someone with inflammatory bowel disease; their only concern was that she shouldn't eat seeds or skins. It seemed that as long as she took the drugs they wanted her to, all would be good. I will never understand the disconnect between conventional medicine and nutrition.

I didn't waste my time arguing with them, but I completely rejected everything they told from a nutrition standpoint. I may not have been well versed yet on all the medications and this new diagnosis, but using food as medicine to integrate into her health plan was something I knew I could handle—or at least I thought I could. In my true fashion, I dove in deep. I was hell-bent on curing her by changing her diet. I went full force, the "rip the Band-Aid off, push you into the deep end, completely all-in" type of crazy. I removed all gluten, refined sugar, and dairy. I made most of her food completely from scratch so that I knew and approved of every single ingredient.

For a while, I even made her own milk with organic almonds or cashews that I soaked and squeezed through a mesh bag. The girls used to laugh and be grossed out when I told them I was busy making milk and straining it through a nut bag, although all the kids ended up loving it. It really is delicious! I bought a separate freezer to keep in the basement that would be just for Ava. I didn't want her to feel like she had to go without, so if she had a craving for something she used to eat, I was bound and determined to create it for her. These recipes were extremely time-consuming to make, not to mention expensive. My grocery bill had nearly doubled, and most of my days were spent in the kitchen. I grew up comfortable in the kitchen, but I honestly couldn't even talk to anyone while making these recipes, as the steps involved required complete concentration. And boy, were there some expensive mistakes. Trust me when I tell you throwing away a small batch of cookies that had fifty dollars' worth of ingredients in them isn't fun.

In hindsight, I know I neglected the rest of my family during this time. I think they all realized what was going on, and they understood. I would have done the same for any of them, but I know there were many times they probably felt brushed aside, ignored, or forgotten about during those first few months of my insanity. Yet at the same time, I also think they didn't fully understand.

I was spread very thin, and my attempts to give equal time were subpar at best. My drive to do what I was doing at that time had a deep, unexplainable purpose that I was powerless to stop. I couldn't verbalize it all, and I think at times many people didn't understand why I wasn't just doing what the doctors told me to do. I was completely overboard, and I knew it. Many, including some of my own family, just didn't understand why I was making this so hard on myself. I was wearing myself out and not giving fair and proper attention to my family. I can understand why that didn't make sense to them; it didn't even fully make sense to me, but I knew that I had to do this, and there was no one who would have been able to stop me.

Over time, I did start to slow down. I got better at cooking, was able to start stockpiling things in the freezer, and found many approved items that I could order to have sent to the house. Ava's inflammatory markers were lowering and the bleeding had finally stopped, so I felt like I could come up for air. It's funny—as I shop now, I see many of these items in grocery stores, but at that time I spent hours searching for these things and paid a fortune to have them shipped. My relentless drive to have her put zero toxins in her body and eat the most nutrient-dense foods would again soon prove that my intuition was on to something, even if my brain would take longer to figure out the reason.

As she was gaining strength, healing, and becoming more familiar with her new lifestyle, some secondary issues began slowly showing up. It began with some aching in her legs. To be quite honest, I was mildly concerned but dismissed it. I knew autoimmune issues could cause things like achy joints, and it wasn't my main concern. After witnessing a severe GI bleed, my focus remained on her gut health. At this point, even though I was a seasoned mom, the list of diagnoses between the girls was growing quite long and getting overwhelming to manage. The Usher syndrome and cochlear implants at this point were even on the backburner, as we had become pretty well versed in all the equipment, appointments, and accommodations that it required.

Ava had also previously been diagnosed with ADHD and had struggled in the past with some anxiety and depression. Each specialist that required follow-ups didn't seem to see the big picture. At times, I wondered how I was even supposed to keep my kids in school and get them to all of these appointments. It had become a full-time job in itself just managing it all and yet here we were again, adding to what seemed to be an ever-growing list of bizarre things. It seemed impossible at times, to be honest, and I never felt like I was adequately giving any of it the time it required.

The leg pain persisted, and Ava's vocalization of it grew stronger with each passing week. At this point, I began asking questions about it. I never really got too much concern from the doctors. No one seemed to think it could be related to her medication, although these strange symptoms slowly started presenting themselves just a few months after starting her immunosuppressive meds, which I was told took a few months to start working. The timing of it all felt strange to me, connected in some way, yet none of her doctors seemed to think so.

I tried several things to alleviate her pain—magnesium lotion, massages, ice, heat, etc. Nothing seemed to ease any of her discomfort, and it seemed things were actually getting progressively worse. The aches shifted to what she described as deep shooting and stabbing bone pain, and her feet had begun to tingle. She had also started requesting mobility aids and purchased herself a cane from Amazon. Something wasn't right.

I scheduled an appointment with a rheumatologist, but it was going to take a few weeks of waiting to get in. I was starting to get anxious. Ava was becoming increasingly tired and slept most days when she got home from school. Weeks later, we left the rheumatologist appointment that day no better off than before. She gave Ava a quick exam and said she had no swelling around her joints, so it didn't appear to be arthritis, and she was unsure of why she was experiencing these symptoms. She suggested we go see a neurologist.

A referral was placed, and again we waited for that appointment to arrive. By this time, Ava started complaining about her hair falling out. We knew this could temporarily happen due to some of the medications she had taken and with how sick she had been. I reminded her that the thinning was probably normal, as her body was reacting to what it had been through three months prior. She was also complaining of feeling lightheaded. Ava told me her heart would race sometimes for no reason at all and at this point, with the leg pain and cane use, she was not doing any form of exercise to elevate it. She also began experiencing random bloody noses. She had never had a bloody nose before in her life, and they were now becoming a frequent occurrence.

We were both looking forward to the upcoming neurology appointment in hopes they would do some testing and be able to give us a reason for what was happening. Not having a reason was the worst part. No explanation meant no hope, no plan for relief. We were beginning to get desperate. After a long exam, neurologist number one came to the conclusion that Ava was depressed and anxious. He explained that I needed to focus on her mental health and seemed to think that once that was managed, all her pains and symptoms would dissipate on their own. I knew I didn't believe him deep down, yet I was so tired of going round and round with no answers, so I allowed a part of me to entertain the idea that maybe he could be right.

We spoke with her psychiatrist, and I agreed to double her Effexor. I was told that increasing the dosage was likely to help with the pain she was experiencing—it did not. And it also didn't help with this so-called "depression" or "anxiety." Instead, Ava complained it made her feel artificial. No one seemed to even consider the idea that there was a reason for her depression and anxiety. Being in pain daily, exhausted, with multiple unexplained symptoms could be reason enough to feel that way. No one seemed to want to figure out the root cause of what was actually happening inside her body to cause this. We proceeded to go round and round, back and forth to specialist after specialist. I can't exactly remember the time frame, but we definitely had gotten used to going to follow-ups, being passed on just to hear the same thing as before, and always being left with no answers and zero relief. We were both beginning to feel quite beaten down.

Finally, we were referred to a children's pain program for an evaluation. I wasn't even sure what that would entail at this point, but it was something we hadn't done yet, so I was willing to try. I hated the thought of pain medication, which is what I expected to be offered, but I had become too desperate to get her some relief and knew I would be willing to entertain the idea.

I tried to go in with an open mind but not to set my expectations too high. I was tired of being let down and dismissed. I was tired of my daughter being in constant pain. But, unexpectedly, this time felt different. There was a team of doctors who all saw her on the same day to evaluate, then strategize as a group to come up with a plan of treatment. Finally, I thought to myself, a group of experts looking at her as a whole, not just a piece of the pie. My daughter was fading away and I had nearly run out of options. I needed some hope, and fast. I felt like maybe, just maybe, we had found our answer.

This neurologist came in and apologized immediately that Ava had previously been dismissed as a psyche problem. I had never had a doctor do that before—an apology from a doctor was something I had never witnessed. He had a different approach and seemed very empathetic. He did a quick evaluation and told me with confidence he knew what Ava had, and he knew how to help.

I couldn't believe what I was hearing. The words I had been waiting to hear for so long flowed into me, and I didn't even think to ask questions. She was diagnosed with amplified musculoskeletal pain syndrome, more commonly referred to as AMPS, and they recommended a three-week inpatient pain program that involved zero drugs. It was based on intense physical therapy, water therapy, group and individual counseling, and a very strict planned-out schedule to reset her pain receptors.

I remember feeling such a weight lifted off my shoulders. I thought, Could this be the answer to our prayers? Finally, a reason, a plan of action, and a way out of this torment we had been living in. Little did I know the misery we had been living in wouldn't even come close to the depths of hell that program would pull us into. I had been fooled again, and my daughter would ultimately pay the price, severely.

CHAPTER 9
THE PAIN PROGRAM

Over fifty thousand dollars was the price of the indoctrination and brainwashing of my child. Money collected to quickly misdiagnose her and take advantage of the pure desperation of a mother caring for a very sick girl. Leaving her there to be watched by strangers feeding her lies, pushing agendas, and keeping secrets from me, all while the true beast inside her was continuing to wreak havoc on her body, will forever haunt me.

The one silver lining was my awakening to the link between conventional medicine, Big Pharma, the pushing of political agendas, and the bullying our government does to silence us out of fear, all in the name of money. Once again, a pattern had emerged.

I am the type of person who needs to experience something firsthand, to really feel something deep down that touches me or someone I love personally, to see a truth that is right in front of me. Every time this happens, I am shocked—shocked because I think my past has taught me better. But I realize now that even with my growth, the devil tries to creep its way in. I am sharper each time, but I will never be immune to the evil of this world. My only hope is to instill my life lessons in my children in hopes that they will be quicker to see it than I was.

The only theory I have come up with that gives me any peace about that time is the realization that God is using me as a vessel. It is what allowed me to finally write this book. That was the missing link I needed to do something I've always wanted to do, but never did because I didn't feel it served the right purpose. I never wanted to share my story just because people were curious about my personal life, or just because someone may find my story interesting. If I ever were to write a book, I needed it to have the potential to open the eyes of those still blindly being led by people who don't actually care about them. I needed my story to help make a difference or create change.

Before the pain program even ended, I knew that my story would eventually be written; I just didn't know when or how. I think back to 2010, during the time after Jeff's death, and I could have told my story on any platform I chose. I could have signed a book deal anytime I wanted. I had reporters and news stations begging for interviews and appearances, but I hadn't wanted any of it. I chose to protect myself and my children as much as I possibly could. Fast forward, and it felt like I was screaming from the rooftops at the top of my lungs, begging someone to listen, and no one would. Life is funny that way, I suppose. Greed masked by interest chooses the stories they want to tell. The stories that make the money, boost the ratings, and push the proper narrative are broadcast to the world, and the ones they don't think will never get told.

When I finally discovered the root cause of my daughter's illness all on my own, I knew the time had come. The pain program was my "ah-ha!" moment. I won't ever say I am grateful for that experience, but I will say that having the opportunity to expose the evil that transpired there will forever be considered a blessing. If even one mind is changed, or if one person is spared from years of suffering by reading this, it will be worth sharing in my eyes.

People traveled from all over the United States to have their child participate in this three-week program. I felt lucky that it was only a short drive from our home. Other families had flown in, rented cars, and were living at the nearby Ronald McDonald House or staying in hotels. I often thought of the sacrifices they made to get their children there, and the planning involved to make it all happen. This is a commitment only a desperate parent who is out of options would make. It was not easy.

Working would not have been an option during this time for at least one parent. The schedules for the kids were very regimented, and it wasn't much different for their caregivers. There were days that I had up to three Zoom calls I needed to participate in spread out throughout the day. We had group parent sessions and individual sessions with all the doctors and therapists treating our children. I remember feeling good about the parent involvement, even though it was overwhelming and time-consuming. It made it feel organized and legit. With this much interaction, I thought, how could there be things happening that parents were not aware of? These were all minor children ranging in age from as young as eight or nine up to seventeen.

I prepared all of Ava's meals in advance. I was not about to let her eat hospital food for three weeks after all she had been through with her ulcerative colitis diagnosis. We were finally getting to a good place as far as gut health was concerned; with all of her latest symptoms, that is the last thing she needed to go south. I spoke with the staff ahead of time and shared my wishes and concerns. They only accepted six children at a time, which allowed for special accommodations, and this accommodation was extremely easy and didn't require any extra work from them. I was told that all her meals would be charted along with her food and water intake. The nutritionist I spoke with wanted to make sure the meals I provided her would be well-balanced. I internally laughed at that—as if somehow my organic grass-fed beef, homemade grain-free treats, and fresh vegetables and fruits would somehow be less nutritious than the menu the hospital provided.

I would bring fresh, wholesome, nutrient-dense, gut-friendly meals down every few days during visiting hours. I spent a fortune and many hours in the kitchen again making sure Ava didn't go without. She had lunch, dinner, desserts, and snacks. After looking at the breakfast options, I informed them that she would be fine ordering bacon and eggs off the menu for that meal. All my prepared meals were separated in containers and labeled with her name and the date. All things she liked, made with immense love and care at home.

I remember one of my first red flags was collecting some of the containers to replace with new ones and seeing some completely full and apparently untouched. I didn't ask too many questions at that point; I just wanted to make sure Ava was eating enough. I knew that I gave her healthy portions and would have rather had too much than not enough. As time went on, however, this seemed to be a regular occurrence.

By this time her inpatient portion was complete and she had moved to the last phase of outpatient treatments, I would drive her there at eight a.m. and pick her up at five p.m. At that point, I sent an email inquiring about my concerns and specifically asked if there was a reason Ava wasn't eating all of her meals. I received a response back saying that after reviewing her charts, it appeared she had been ordering off the menu. I was furious.

I was not only mad at them—I was mad at Ava. It felt like a slap in the face for all my efforts. But she was a child, a sick child dealing with intense pain on a daily basis. She was depressed and tired. I'm sure at that point in time, she didn't even think about the ramifications of her choices. Ordering crap off the menu probably made her feel good for at least the fifteen minutes it took to eat. Like any kid pushing the boundaries, she probably assumed she would give it a try and expected to be shut down.

Ava was extremely compliant with her new way of eating at home and actually enjoyed it. However, we didn't really have a lot of options for her to be tempted by, either. The fact that this was overlooked, deemed unimportant, and allowed was unbelievable to me. She was in the facility because she needed help. They were in charge, not her! This negligence caused me to begin to dig deeper.

The woman in charge of nutrition acted like it was no big deal. This is the woman whom I had multiple conversations and exchanged emails with about Ava's diet. We had thoroughly discussed the details and logistics, and she had agreed to my wishes. As a nutritionist, it seemed she was intelligent enough to understand and appreciate my attention to detail regarding her gut health while she was away, but it appeared I had put too much faith in her to execute her responsibilities correctly.

Her response was that she had figured if Ava was ordering off the menu, then it was okay for her to eat. She had assumed Ava was in the right mental state to make that choice for herself and was somehow aware of all the ingredients of each menu item. That was it. I had placed Ava in their care, a place where she didn't get a choice of what she did during the day because they followed such a strict schedule, and was assured my wishes concerning her diet would be followed. They were not, and again, she paid the price, and I was left to be responsible for facilitating the necessary measures needed to rectify this mistake.

I had her calprotectin levels tested again shortly after and they had increased from 27 to over 800. Her GI doctor recommended switching from azathioprine to a biologic called Humira. According to her, the first drug was no longer doing its job. I knew at this point no medical professional would ever entertain the idea that her diet of hospital nuggets, pizza, and French fries could have contributed to this, but I knew better. Yet, I agreed to the medication change, as I was extremely fearful of the damage this amount of inflammation could do. I didn't think either of us could have handled a repeat of the last hospital stay.

During her day treatment, my sister and I had planned to spend some time with a childhood friend who had moved to Ohio for her husband's job in the Coast Guard. Kathy was technically my sister's friend, but I had also grown up with her. She lived within ten minutes of the facility Ava was being treated at and she offered her home as a place to relax, take my Zoom calls, and lessen my driving back and forth.

Kathy was the one who was actually responsible for me seeing Jeff for the first time. Back in high school, she had gotten my sister and I jobs at Michigan International Speedway during NASCAR season working as waitresses in the infield suites. Jeff was working as a tent, table, and chairs guy. I will always consider that place as special. We never spoke during our summers there, but it was the first time we ever locked eyes.

Kathy is the type of person you can share anything with, no matter how many years have gone by. I've always admired her quirky and hardcore ways. Kathy definitely knows who she is, how she wants to parent, and what she believes in, and it changes for no one, ever. She is extremely grounded in her faith and isn't afraid to show it. She's extremely accepting but will be the first to question your choices, and she always makes me laugh. There is nothing off-limits with her, and I don't think she knows what the word "embarrassed" means. At this point, it had been years since I had seen her in person.

As we got caught up, we reminisced about the event that took place the last time we were all together. She now has five children, but at that time she had only three. We joke that I am responsible for her fourth.

Kathy was in a place at that time where she wasn't feeling very confident in her own skin. I think motherhood in general, as it does, had worn her out. It was time for her to prioritize her own self-maintenance. We were planning to meet up at my sister's house for a visit with our kids, and I was really looking forward to seeing her since it had been such a long time. Kathy was very aware of my background in cosmetology. I had gone to beauty school when I was laid off as a flight attendant after 9/11 in Aberdeen, Mississippi, while Jeff was in undergraduate pilot training. I had always done my friends' highlights, a quick haircut, or a wax.

Apparently, Kathy was in need of a wax and asked me to bring my supplies. I happily obliged, not totally understanding the wax she was referring to. With our kids happily watching a show in my sister's bedroom, we laid out the necessities in her bathroom. We already had tears in our eyes as she had explained how long it had been since this region had had maintenance of any kind. This was the type of friendship we had, though, so I never thought for a second to decline this request. And without getting into too much detail, I will say this was a pretty time-consuming job. I think I was actually sweating at one point and had to pull my hair back into a ponytail.

I don't think I have ever laughed harder in my life than the days my sister and I spent with Kathy during Ava's day visits at the pain clinic. Kathy is always good for the kind of laugh that you can feel aching in your stomach even days later. The kind of laughter that makes you forget about anything bad going on in your life. The kind of laughter that truly heals, even if for just a little bit. After the swelling went down from the work I put in that day, sure enough, baby number four was conceived.

That day after dropping Ava off, I began filling Kathy in on the uneasy feeling I was getting about this program and she instantly saw red flags. She and my sister quietly listened in on my Zoom calls that day, hearing my concerns and how they were being handled. I saw Kathy grab a pen and paper and start feverishly writing things down. I could barely concentrate as her two bulldogs aggressively licked each other on the couch right next to where my sister was trying to relax. Kelly and I kept looking at each other in disgust, but Kathy wasn't fazed at all. At times I would have to hit the mute button, as I was sure the people on the other end could hear it. Little did I know that the way my computer was facing, they not only heard but could probably see it for themselves.

After that call ended, she explained jokingly that they were lesbian sisters and she was just so used to it, it barely fazed her anymore. Apparently they never stopped, and she had given up trying to make them. We belly laughed again so damn hard while clutching our stomachs and, as expected, my midsection hurt for days. I never expected to be laughing that hard during a time of such turmoil. But it happened, and it felt so good. I also left that day feeling validated by their responses to my concern. Something wasn't right about what had happened there, and I was bound and determined to find out what it was.

As Ava transitioned back home, we had a very intense and specific schedule we were supposed to stick to. There would be zero naps during the day, no matter how tired she was. There would be specific exercises to complete daily, and I was not, for any reason, to ask her about her pain. I was told not to do extra things for her, and to not have her siblings pick up her slack. It had something to do with secondary gains and bringing extra attention to her pain. I agreed for a while. At that point, I honestly thought that maybe the program had helped, despite the fact that they had disregarded everything I said about Ava's meals. She didn't seem to be complaining about being in pain and was fairly compliant with the schedule.

As I was looking over her discharge paperwork, I kept seeing the same thing written down. "Patient presents with zero pain." I remembered back to when I was researching and how high the success rate of the program was. A lightbulb went off.

I broke down and told Ava my feelings and how it just didn't feel right to me to follow their rules. I apologized to her for letting strangers talk me into going against my motherly instincts, and that's when she told me they had told her not to mention or talk about her pain as well. These poor kids were being brainwashed into thinking they couldn't speak up if they were hurting, and the parents were privately told the same thing. I'll never know for sure, but that sounds like a pretty clever way to get that great success percentage rate. And at over $50,000 per child, it seemed to be a great financial gain as well.

The truth was that Ava wasn't better. She was not pain-free. In fact, she was getting worse. At this point, she was asking me for a walker to replace her cane. Mobility aids were not allowed at the pain program and I had repeatedly been told to avoid them, so I was very hesitant. I think the only thing that actually calmed her nervous system at that time was the conversation we'd had. The sense of relief in her eyes when I told her we were going to talk about her pain was almost as intense as the hug she gave me after.

As Ava continued to go downhill, I felt I was back at square one. More doctors' appointments were scheduled. I was back to not only researching possible causes, but investigating and thumbing through her pain program binder and online medical charts with a fine-tooth comb. I sent multiple messages to her primary care provider requesting actual diagnostic testing. At this point in time, I needed to start ruling everything out, even if it seemed far-fetched. She was extremely apprehensive and just kept placing referrals for us to see doctors we had already seen.

We did, however, have a new appointment coming up with a pediatric cardiologist who would be evaluating Ava due to her random heart rate spikes and constantly being lightheaded. Once, she even passed out in the shower. After lifting her naked body off the floor, I eventually got her a shower chair. She was now sitting while showering to prevent injury from a possible fall.

I brought my crumpled piece of paper with all of my notes and crazy ideas that could be possible causes of Ava's ailments to show him. Any chance I got to run my thoughts by someone new, I took. He did an EKG and echocardiogram on her and they came back normal. However, I think he could tell that something wasn't right. He politely took my list, sat down, removed his mask, and really looked at it. He was so kind, empathetic, and smart. Not smart in an egotistical way, as some doctors can be, just down-to-earth.

My list of possibilities had started leaning more toward environmental things. With each doctor we saw who had no answers, my drive to dig deeper grew stronger. At this point, most of my lists consisted of things that made doctors look at me like I was crazy—chemical sensitivities, mold, poisons, water contamination, psittacosis, or anything she could have picked up working at the pet store.

I'll never forget the moment he stopped reading and looked up at me. "This isn't my area of expertise here, but I really think your list is worth looking into." He paused for a second and followed up with, "I shouldn't be saying this, but it may be time for you to look elsewhere for a second opinion." He said his only other recommendation would be to perhaps visit immunology and infectious disease specialists, and he placed those referrals for me. He also asked me if I was a doctor myself. He said my word usage and condensed, straight-to-the-point extreme knowledge of every single aspect of her issues made him believe that I was. I simply smiled and said, "No, I'm not, I am just a desperate mother who refuses to stop until I get answers." I will never forget him. He was one of the kindest doctors I have ever encountered.

Ava's tingling feet had now turned numb and her right foot had started to drag. She stayed home more than she went to school, and if she did go, it was common for me to get a call from the nurse saying I needed to come pick her up. She was more fatigued than ever, her brain fog had become increasingly prominent, her long hair that she had chopped off the day after the pain clinic was still thinning, and there were constant texts from school while she was stuck in the bathroom trying to stop a nosebleed. I started worrying about her hurting herself. She had stated to me numerous times how she'd rather be dead than feel this way. I knew she didn't like the way she looked. She was never the most confident girl, but ever since Curt, things had gotten worse. And after the pain program, it seemed as though she had grown even more uncomfortable in her body.

There was a specific therapist at the pain clinic who I'd had some especially unpleasant encounters with. Something about her rubbed me the wrong way. Her political views couldn't be hidden and they would ooze out unsuspectingly to others, but I quickly caught on. After talking with Ava and getting a few tidbits of what transpired during their one-on-one sessions, I quickly requested all of her medical records and psychotherapy notes. At this point, I was waking up during the night daily to check on Ava. I couldn't sleep unless I saw her chest rise and fall, and I could never admit it at the time, but I had flashes of myself walking into her room and seeing something horrific that would tell me this all was more than she could take.

You can imagine my surprise to discover—only while reading through her medical records—that she had been placed on a moderate suicide watch during her time at the pain clinic, based off of her initial intake questions. She had also told them that she had access to guns in our home. I found all this out after she had come home, on my own. That part wasn't true, but they didn't know that. We do have guns in our home, but they are locked and secured, and she certainly doesn't have access to them. You would think that alone would have warranted an immediate call home. A heads-up to inform me of this extremely important information, a check-in to make sure that our guns were secured in a locked safe, and a reminder to keep an extra close eye on her. Information like that should be mandatory to share with the parent of a minor. Thank God nothing happened, but if something had, wouldn't they be somehow liable?

I also found that she had suffered a panic attack while there after witnessing another patient suffer a seizure during dinner with no staff around. Her chart stated that her therapist had been called and briefed, but I was not. Here I was spending hours per day on Zoom calls discussing pain management strategies, yet very pertinent information regarding the safety and well-being of my child was purposely being withheld from me.

I also discovered an exercise in her binder that was done in a group therapy session. It was an "All About Me" worksheet. There were four squares to be filled in with "things that make me, me." The odd thing about this was that it also came with a pie chart of suggestions. You would think the suggestions for that age group would be something along the lines of "creative," "helpful," "a good friend," or "hardworking." Instead, there were prompts for things like race, income, sexual orientation, and gender identity, putting ideas in their heads that maybe their pain had something to do with what color they were, or if they were poor, then maybe their pain was somehow worse.

And as far as discussing sexual preference and gender identity with minor children was concerned, I couldn't find one single reason that would make that discussion okay. In fact, it seemed predatory, and something that I would have warned my children about. An adult should never be speaking to children about these sorts of things, ever, especially without the knowledge or permission of the parent.

I had also come to find out that this program—which was a part of the hospital system I have taken my children to for years—admitted to practicing gender-affirming care with all their patients. I was told it was respectful, and that all children were asked if they wanted to use a name other than what was listed on their chart and if they had any preferred pronouns. Ava had a list of diagnoses a mile long, but gender dysphoria was not one of them. I wasn't sure of the motive behind not only discussing but suggesting these things to young minds that were already struggling—and without the knowledge, permission, or consent of a parent.

The strange thing is that I personally was never asked these questions. I was assumed to be female and referred to as only "she" or "her," and Ava was never asked these questions in front of me. The secretive nature is what made my blood boil the most.

How would it ever be deemed appropriate to allude to a struggling child that their pain could be due to being born into the wrong body or how much money their parents have? In my opinion, they were meddling where they didn't belong. Attempting to socially transition children behind the backs of their parents? It seemed like the age of consent and parental rights were slowly becoming a thing of the past.

A social transition can be a gateway to the medicalization, sterilization, and mutilation of these young confused minds that could tie them to the pharmaceutical companies for life, and that is something parents most definitely should be involved in. We all know the amount of money that would generate. It was all starting to make sense to me. Silence people out of fear, brainwash them with ideologies, make feelings more important than the truth, and poison them with food, water, and products riddled with toxins to keep them alive, yet sick enough to need a bucketful of prescriptions and plenty of doctors' appointments.

I've never cared personally what an adult of sound mind chooses to do in the bedroom or in a surgical center. What I do care about is the agenda to push this on children who are not developed enough to make these sorts of permanent life-altering decisions, especially children who are suffering in pain every day and mentally affected by it. Covid allowed it into their bedrooms via social media, and now doctors and therapists are being trained to essentially suggest and affirm instead of trying to find the root cause of their mental and physical pain. I had had enough, and Ava had endured enough. The fire that had ignited in me was in full force, and I realized clearly for the first time that I was on my own here.

"**B**efore you can kill the monster, you have to say its name." Ava sent me this quote by author Terry Pratchett in the midst of her struggles. Reading it now gives me chills. I didn't realize it at the time, but this quote could literally sum up my entire life, and it certainly captures the essence of this time in hers pretty perfectly. My life had consisted of many monsters that needed to be identified and eradicated; this was no different. I would persist until I won, but I first needed to discover its name.

By this time, I was almost certain that Ava's issues were stemming from something in her environment. I had finally pushed hard enough for her to receive some imaging and also an EMG test that measures muscle response or electrical activity response to a nerve's stimulation of the muscle. The tests showed no smoking guns, but I was happy to cross them off my list. While I was waiting for our upcoming appointment with an infectious disease doctor, I made an appointment with a functional medicine practitioner Nick's sister had recommended. Her personal background and knowledge in this area was significant, and I always trusted her suggestions and opinions. I just wish I had listened sooner when she suggested this route.

As my options for answers dwindled, I decided a thorough deep clean of her bedroom was a good idea. I had plans to move her temporarily to the basement so I could fully gut and clean her bedroom and remove the carpet. The more I researched, I kept stumbling upon something called chronic inflammatory response syndrome (CIRS), a progressive multisystem illness characterized by exposure to biotoxins. When reading about how CIRS can affect virtually any body part or organ system of the body and how it can become debilitating if left untreated, I just had a gut feeling I was narrowing in on the root cause of Ava's misery. This diagnosis would make perfect sense in so many ways, I thought.

I knew Ava's genetic makeup made her more sensitive to things, and her MTHFR gene didn't allow detox to always happen efficiently. Methylenetetrahydrofolate is an enzyme that breaks down the amino acid homocysteine, and it can contribute to a variety of health conditions. It is a gene mutation that interferes with the body's proper methylation system, which also means the body does not naturally detox properly. These mysterious symptoms all started after her immunosuppressant meds had kicked in that lowered her body's natural ability to fight off infections and toxins. I knew I was on to something here; I just didn't know exactly what it was.

Nick had piqued my interest when he showed me an article about potential negative effects of bird droppings that could be inhaled and cause sickness. I had purchased a Quaker parrot for Ava for her sixteenth birthday. She named him Wasabi, and I bought him from a very reputable breeder. I figured I would start with him, as there was nothing I could initially think of in our home that could be causing this.

I made an appointment with the avian vet nearby, and I told him everything and explained that money was not a concern. I was not going to half-ass anything—I needed to be one hundred percent thorough in my endeavors. I wanted Wasabi tested for anything and everything that could be potentially harming Ava. While we were waiting for his results, I made an appointment to have our water tested. Wasabi's tests came back and he was the picture of health, and I knew Ava was relieved. That little bird, though much noisier than I anticipated, has helped her through some very hard times. I crossed that off the list and kept moving forward. Our water, as expected, was not what you would call the greatest. I booked an install that day to have a reverse osmosis system put in.

While we were waiting for that, I completed our consultation with the functional medicine practitioner, filled her in on Ava's story, and booked our first appointment. I also started swapping out the rest of our household products that I had not yet changed out for cleaner options. I decided to purchase and replace anything that could potentially have mold in it, such as the washer, dryer, dishwasher, and vacuum. I went old-school with a Riccar vacuum with clean air technology that delivered advanced filtration using a HEPA self-sealing charcoal bag recommended for people with allergies. I was determined to leave no stone unturned.

I also decided that I wanted to test the air in our home. There was no reason to believe our home was unhealthy, and even I had many questions as to why I was considering this extreme measure. There were no musty smells or water damage, no visible mold or areas of concern. Again, I just had a very strong gut feeling. And I didn't just want it tested like they do during a home inspection—I wanted someone well versed in environmental illness who would test every single room in our entire house.

I found a company with a machine called the InstaScope. Traditional air samples use a spore trap cassette with a pump that pulls air over a glass slide with adhesive to trap spores. These tests get sent out to a lab and are reviewed under a microscope. This machine I wanted, however, quantifies airborne mold in real time, providing instant results. This technology was originally developed to detect anthrax in airports, train stations, and other facilities after the terrorist attacks of 9/11. Reading the results in real time would allow me to walk around with the operator and watch the numbers rise and fall, which would lead us directly to the source of the problem if there was one.

While we waited for the air quality inspection, we visited with the infectious disease doctor. I told him all of my concerns and all of Ava's symptoms and begged him to run a mold and fungal lab on her. He refused. Instead, he lectured me for twenty minutes about getting her another meningitis vaccination due to the fact that she had cochlear implants. He also reminded me that she should have the Covid vaccine and her flu shot. Ava was literally dying, and he was only concerned with pumping her with more toxins that I didn't think her body could handle. I knew that was the last thing I would be doing, but I just sat there, defeated, and listened to him. Knowing yet again we had been let down and dismissed made me feel even sadder.

He explained that Ava had zero respiratory issues and, after evaluating her, he saw no reason to believe she needed to be tested for those things. The only thing he agreed on was a urine test for histoplasmosis. I didn't ask for the test, but he stated that due to the fact that she was taking Humira and it was prevalent in the soil in the central and eastern states, particularly the Ohio and Mississippi River Valleys, he would agree to it. It was negative.

Ava seemed indifferent during most appointments. She was exhausted from explaining her story, and at this point she had given up that anyone would help her. She would sit on the exam table, allow them to check her out, and answer the same questions over and over again, looking sad, depleted, and scared. She had lost hope, and maybe even at times she could sense my defeat, though I tried to hide it. She hated these appointments and didn't want to go. I felt guilty dragging her to them all, and I knew she didn't believe me anymore when I told her that eventually someone would know what to do, and we just had to keep going until we found them.

Not long after, we went to our very first functional medicine appointment. This was a place that addressed root cause issues, not just symptoms. It's a science-based approach to addressing the underlying causes of disease. My only regret was not taking her sooner! It was an immense sacrifice to take her there, as insurance was not accepted and everything was out of pocket. I had already spent approximately $25,000 out of pocket on replacing things around the house and her alternative therapies. I knew functional medicine would cost anywhere between $200 and $400 per hour, and that didn't include the testing, supplements, and nutrition. By this point, I didn't care; I knew I would find a way, no matter what the cost. It was overwhelming, but I put my anxiety about the money on the backburner. I wasn't yet aware that by the end of it all, the cost would be eight times that amount.

Ava's practitioner was a beautiful woman with blonde hair and skin that radiated health. She had a warmth in her eyes, a kind smile, and a calming voice. I loved how she looked at Ava and asked her questions first. She immediately made Ava feel important. Ava can be shy and although I don't always like to, I typically talk for her at most doctors' appointments, especially the ones we were used to going to.

Every time, I knew we had less than fifteen minutes to try to get out absolutely every detail possible that would somehow be convincing enough to make someone give a shit. I had learned quickly how to speak fast and efficiently. I had my speech perfected, and it was like literal word vomit at a thousand miles per hour, just hoping that something I said would spark some interest or empathy, but it never did. This time was distinctly different.

This practitioner had worked in conventional medicine for years until she became a patient herself, diagnosed with breast cancer. It wasn't until then that she realized her desire and passion to search for what truly defines our health, to make a difference using an integrated approach that didn't just treat symptoms, but dug deep for the root cause of the issue. She spent almost two hours with Ava that day and talked to Ava like she was the only thing in the world that mattered. Ava soaked in her caring demeanor while sipping on a Mexican hot chocolate made with almond milk from the cafe there.

The office was beautiful, and we both felt instantly calm when we entered. It was a little piece of heaven right here in Ohio. It is multiple businesses, all women-owned, that work as a unit promoting mental, emotional, physical, and spiritual health. And there was food! Like, really, really good food, organic, gluten-free, and locally sourced. It's truly a gem. At a time when Ava's future seemed harrowing and my list of options had become extremely short, it felt magical.

I looked at Ava as we walked inside that first visit. We didn't even have to speak; we could both feel it. We both knew instantly when our eyes met that this was the place where she would begin to heal. I would have sold all my possessions to pay the bill for this incredible unicorn of a healing mecca.

Ava cried during that intake appointment. It was the first time she had ever truly felt heard in a medical setting. Every appointment up until that point, she looked lifeless, lethargic, and very sick, with nothing behind her eyes. Many times, it felt like I was taking a frail old lady at the end of her life to the doctor. The emotion she allowed to spill out of her blue eyes that day gave me so much hope. Afterward, we had lunch right there at their little restaurant, where everything was made just as I had made at home for her, but better. She had so many choices of wholesome, nutritious food to pick from. She had a grilled chicken sandwich on a gluten-free bun with sweet potato chips, and everything was clean and nutritious. It was the first time in almost two years I had seen a glimmer of hope in her eyes.

We discussed the testing that would be ordered for her and started some supplements for her to start taking while we waited for the results. Leaving that day, we both knew we had finally found what we had been desperately searching for. We were home, and I felt like the whole world might have heard the sigh of relief that left my body that day.

A few weeks later, the day of the InstaScope test was upon us. It was a large, awkward, and heavy machine. The man conducting the test was extremely knowledgeable about mold and toxins and was everything I had been looking for. He invited Nick and I to follow him around and explained exactly how everything worked. He started by testing the air outside our home so we had a comparison, informing us that every house has mold; 6,000 parts per million or less is considered acceptable. He explained that for people with autoimmune issues or a suppressed immune system, though, the home should be 4,000 parts per million or less to be safe. He started in our downstairs storage room where the HVAC system is. His eyes widened as we watched the numbers start to soar. We had 80,000 parts per million over our HVAC system—the lungs of the house, pumping through the ducts filtering mycotoxins out to each and every vent in our home.

I knew this was awful—and the severity of what would need to be done to our home had not yet registered—but I honestly could have cried tears of joy. At last, I knew I had finally found the root cause of Ava's suffering—I had done what I set out to do. I had given her my word that I would not stop until I found the answer, and on that day, I was certain I had fulfilled my promise. I felt validated and full of hope. This was the day I had dropped to my knees and prayed so many times. I think only God himself could have given me the strength to persist through the chains of all the skeptics and doubters trying to drag me down.

I had experienced many secondary losses during this phase of my life as well, and I was grateful my skin was thicker now. I can be too much for some people. I am well aware of this and completely okay with it. This had become my life. Illness, caregiving, researching, agendas, politics, toxins, and sickness—it was all I talked about, and I knew it wasn't a fun subject most of the time.

I was more prepared this time around, though, and I honestly didn't care at all. As I become more outspoken about toxins, environmental illness, politics, vaccines, ideologies, and honestly just speaking the truth, I had many people unfriend me or magically become distant. It was sad in a way, because I have always been able to have friends with opinions or lifestyles different from mine; it can work quite well when there is mutual respect. Sadly, I think that is fading away in our current society. When you completely shut people out because they don't share your same beliefs, you create an even bigger divide. I have always welcomed a respectful conversation on a hot topic, as I truly care about learning why someone feels the way that they do. And I also welcome the opportunity to perhaps educate them on my own story and how my past has significantly shaped my views on this world.

I even had one woman whom I considered a friend unfriend me on social media for what I can only assume was because I started having the confidence to post my opinion on controversial topics. I had known for years that most of her political beliefs differed greatly from mine, as she was always outspoken about them, but it never bothered me. I really enjoyed her as a person and thought she was wickedly talented and creative. I had always supported her business and, unbeknownst to her, paid for one of her children's extracurricular activities while her husband was going through a hard time medically because I knew there was a financial strain on her family. I still don't regret doing that, and it's probably for the best that she doesn't even know it was me.

This is just one story; there are many more. But none of those losses mattered to me. I had finally found the answer I had been seeking, and it was time to get to work. I knew we had a fight ahead to heal, but at that moment, I truly felt the victory of the most brutal battle I had ever fought.

As the InstaScope machine continued along the basement, the man followed the numbers down the hallway. As we slowly approached the first bedroom, they began to climb even higher. He entered Vinny's playroom and let his wand lead him closer to our crawl space, which was located in the closet of this room accessed by a small ladder. His machine read over 400,000 parts per million. These were lethal levels—and the highest he had ever seen. He told me immediately that if I would have moved Ava downstairs while I redid her bedroom, it probably would have killed her. At that moment, I could only believe that some divine intervention had taken place. I'd like to think it was her father, perhaps alongside God himself.

At this point, the man wouldn't even continue testing the air until he went back to his truck to get an N95 mask. After he put it on, he persisted until every space in our home had been tested. Luckily, due to the placement of what we now refer to as "ground zero"—the furnace—our main living area seemed to have been spared as well as our office, which was located toward the front of our home. Vinny's bedroom was also spared, perhaps due to the way the house was vented and that it was new construction. Stella's room had higher than normal counts, and poor Ava's room was reading at over 10,000 parts per million.

I thought about how sick she had been over the past year. She didn't leave the house much at all; she would stay up in her room most days, with the door closed, and sleep. All this time, she had been in that enclosed room being infiltrated with massive amounts of mycotoxins invading her already immune-compromised body. I remember Ava's eyes growing wide and intense when I told her we had done it. The look on her face when I informed her we had discovered what I believed to be the root cause of her pain and suffering was one of shock and pure relief. She hugged me and let out a deep, long exhale. I told her it was going to be okay, and I felt like she finally believed me.

That very day, we purchased brand-new mattresses, bedding, and essentials for the kids. We cleared out the office/workout room and welcomed all three kids into the makeshift bedroom that they would be sharing indefinitely. I sent Wasabi to the bird hotel and banned the kids from entering the upstairs and the basement. Ground zero was completely sealed off, and the inspector had advised us not to even open the basement door without an N95. He assured me that this room would be safe for them to sleep in, coming in at less than 3,000 parts per million. I figured it was the best we could do for the time being until we figured out exactly what it would entail to remediate our home properly.

I had previously read that 25 percent of the human population has a genetic makeup that doesn't allow them to detox properly. Add in immune-suppressant medication and an autoimmune disease, and you don't have a fighting chance.

We had experienced a burst pipe approximately eight years prior from an outside faucet. It was examined by an insurance adjuster immediately, and we were given the name of a restoration company to contact. We got a hold of them right away and remediation took place fairly quickly. The leak had been in the basement bedroom—which had been used as Vinny's playroom until this realization—where the crawl space is located.

The water had come into our home about three feet over from the crawl space through a ceiling tile. The restoration company had seemed thorough to us. They drilled holes in the walls, completely dried everything out, and our floors and baseboards were completely replaced. Other than the inconvenience of it all and the few items we had needed to throw away, all seemed to be alright. It had all been covered by insurance, and we believed that they had taken all the right precautions and followed the proper steps correctly. Boy, were we so very wrong. Apparently, the water in the crawl space had never been detected.

I immediately called our insurance company to file a claim and sent the InstaScope reports to them. They then sent another adjustor out, who told us that the undetected water that had been growing toxic mold had most definitely stemmed from the burst pipe. There would have been no other avenue for it to be water damaged. At this point, after receiving the plan of action and the estimate of the cost, I felt a little relieved, fairly confident our insurance company would take care of the remediation. Again, I was terribly mistaken.

According to the insurance company, the statute of limitations was one year after the original remediation took place. We would have had to report a problem within one year to have anything covered. The problem with that, of course, was that we didn't know. There was nothing visible to us that would have indicated a problem with their work. The remediation attempts that were done had been executed correctly; we were not aware they had failed to detect water in the crawl space. We don't use that crawl space at all. At that time, it was filled with bins and things I had put there when the girls and I had moved into the house that belonged to their father.

I had placed these things inside the crawl space for safekeeping, thinking that when the girls were older, they would want to go through everything themselves. They had been far too young when he died for me to decide what would have meaning to them and what wouldn't. So, I kept everything. Now, the thought of having to throw it all in the garbage was unbearable. Notebooks from his college years, photographs, flight manuals with his handwritten notes in the margins, and more all needed to be tossed in the giant dumpster in our driveway. I didn't even have the heart to tell them.

In the end, getting any assistance was met with a hard no from the insurance company. But they did send me twenty bucks for the replacement of the one Styrofoam ceiling panel they had ruined during their inspection. Once again, we were completely on our own.

The remediation company we'd hired to rid our house of mold had a plan. They would use containment barriers to avoid any cross contamination, along with HEPA-filtered air filtration devices to create negative pressure in the containment area during the process. We would need to find other living arrangements while this process was being completed, and we were advised to purge anything that was porous; they would be able to treat any hard nonporous item. This was critical, as there was no way to remove every single mycotoxin out of anything permeable.

As sick as Ava was, along with the scary fact that we knew these toxins were living inside all of us, we followed their advice meticulously. We had a large dumpster delivered. We had a week to coordinate everything that needed to be done prior to remediation. We all took a condensed version of the time it took to process throwing away almost our entire home, including precious memories and some irreplaceable things, and went to work. I just told myself over and over, as I stuffed black garbage bags full of my past and present, that nothing in this world was more important than the health of my family.

Ava is an artist and an avid reader, and unfortunately we needed to take the biggest precautions in her room. She was teary-eyed to find out that her entire collection of books, artwork, journals, and any keepsakes that were nonporous would need to be thrown away. I allowed her to come upstairs with a mask on to witness it. She understood why it had to happen, but I could see the internal heartbreak of losing all the things that made her feel like her. She was so sad. Stella is a collector of beautiful bedding and luxurious blankets, and she had a few stuffed animals she needed to throw away. She was disappointed but very grown-up about the situation; she never complained.

We were able to send away a few precious things to a restoration company that would decontaminate and ozone them, but it was extremely expensive. We needed to be very selective with what we chose. These items included their dad's flight jacket, his baby pillow named Poody, and of course, all of the kids' favorite stuffies from childhood. Stella's Snuggie, Ava's bunny, and Vincent's Crinky were all sent to be restored.

Vinny thankfully didn't have to get rid of much from his room due to the mycotoxin count being within normal range. He was, however, quite upset about all of our special decorations and things in his playroom that he needed to say goodbye to. I don't think he really understood why we were doing all of these things, and he did ask me once if he would get sick, too. I tried to explain why some people get sick and others don't, but it was hard for him. He did enjoy the time he got to spend rooming with his sisters, though.

It took three large dumpsters to hold the parts of our life that were toxic. That didn't include furniture; the remediation company would handle removing all of the large items and all of the carpet in our home. Thankfully, I did have some much-needed help with our part. My neighbor Roxanne showed up one morning with rubber gloves and an N95 mask. I held the large garbage bags, and she stuffed years of bedding, blankets, holiday decor, and our life into them. Everything in the crawl space had to go. All of Jeff's papers, flight manuals, flight suits, and clothes that I had saved for the girls were going in the garbage. I was beyond relieved that my wedding dress, his flight jacket, and his funeral flags were not in that space and were able to be sent out to be cleaned properly.

Kelly and I spent hours in Ava's room. We purged and we separated. We had her favorite clothes and a few irreplaceable things sent off to a company that would decontaminate and ozone them, and the pile we originally created to send away was quoted at $25,000 just to clean. We were able to dwindle that down to a total of $7,000. Deciding what stays in and goes out of your life, to put a price tag on these special items, was excruciating. So, as you can imagine, we could only send what was absolutely irreplaceable.

We cleaned each and every nonporous item with a hospital-grade disinfectant cleaner, including what was probably three hundred pieces of handmade jewelry Ava had created during the past few years. Art, jewelry making, and crochet were hobbies she'd picked up when she was no longer well enough to stay a part of her competitive judo team. All cleaned items were sealed in plastic bags, and everything else was hauled downstairs and tossed in the dumpster.

By the weekend, our home looked nearly empty. It was prepared for the removal of the silent killer that had been secretly growing in hiding for eight years. A hotel had been booked, the dogs boarded. By this point we had administered all the lab testing, including a mycotoxin test for Ava, and were anxiously awaiting the results. We handed over the keys to our home and prayed that when we returned, it would be a healthy home—and a place for Ava to heal.

Finally, we received an e-mail that Ava had new test results to review. As I logged into her portal, I felt nervous. Pictures of the past few years flashed in my mind. Images of toilets filled with blood, her weak naked body passed out on the shower floor, her clumps of hair collected from the drain. I had flashbacks of my now wheelchair-bound daughter walking up to a fight on the judo mat, strong and confident just a few years prior. I took a deep breath in, held it for three seconds, and exhaled. It was time.

I clicked on her MycoTOX profile and there it was, staring right at me. The final bit of evidence, the confirmation that proved the power of maternal instincts and pure determination. Extremely high levels of aspergillus, ochratoxin A, citrinin, and dihydrocodeinone DHC were in her body.

Ochratoxin A is a nephrotoxic, immunotoxic, and carcinogenic mycotoxin. Exposure occurs primarily through water-damaged buildings. As I read further, I learned it can lead to kidney disease and adverse neurological effects. Some studies had even shown it may contribute to neurodegenerative diseases such as Alzheimer's and Parkinson's. There have been studies conducted that showed significant oxidative damage to multiple brain regions, and it is highly nephrotoxic. Citrinin is produced by the mold aspergillus, penicillium, and monascus. Her results stated the most common exposure routes were through ingestion, inhalation, and skin contact. Citrinin's ability to increase the permeability of mitochondrial membranes in the kidneys can lead to nephropathy. It is carcinogenic and has been linked to immune suppression.

As I sat there and read, I couldn't help but think of the endless lists of doctors I had taken her to, all the messages I had sent begging for testing, and all the desperate calls I had made on a regular basis fearing for my daughter's life, pleading for help.

Pediatricians, gastroenterologists, rheumatologists, neurologists, cardiologists, psychologists, nutritionists, psychiatrists, ER visits, and a full team of doctors at the pain program. These were the best of the best, doctors at a world-renowned hospital. Yet over the course of a two-year span, none of these doctors were able to figure out what was wrong with Ava.

Not one of them seemed to care enough to dig deeper. Even when I had been doing all the research and pretty much handed it right to them, they still refused and didn't believe me. Aside from the cardiologist who listened enough to tell me to keep pushing forward with my instincts, all of them believed this to be psychosomatic, all in her head, and brushed her off to the next specialist or suggested counseling.

The cardiologist said something to me I will never forget: He told me he always listens to mothers when they have a gut instinct, even if it sounds far-fetched. He was the only one who got it. Unfortunately, he could only run so many tests under his specialty, and he did. Aside from him, every single one of them were all too wrapped up in their bubble of conventional medicine to even think for a second that someone's mother might know more than they do.

CHAPTER 11
COMING BACK TO LIFE

While writing this chapter, I'm listening to the Pink Floyd song "Coming Back to Life." Pink Floyd was a favorite of Jeff's. This one in particular was always a favorite, and the words really resonated with me as I thought about the previous few years and all that had transpired.

Ava's new functional medicine practitioner, who had become the only provider I trusted, put together a plan immediately. She wanted to go nice and slow. Ava's body had become so sensitive, she didn't want to overwhelm her. We started by removing the foods that tests indicated she was reactive to. Then she prescribed the proper gut supplements to help heal her microbiome and a few others for things she was deficient in. We started at one-eighth of the recommended dosage of a binder that consisted of activated charcoal, zeolite, bentonite clay, and aloe vera leaf. Binders work like a magnet, attracting toxins from within the body to be flushed out. In order to flush them out, your detox pathways need to be open and working properly. The problem with someone as sick as Ava was that hers were not.

She was not having regular bowel movements and she wasn't sweating at all, ever. If you take too much of a binder, there is a risk of something called a Herxheimer reaction, where the binder pulls the toxins out faster than your body can eliminate them and causes a person to feel worse. Fever, chills, nausea and vomiting, low blood pressure, tachycardia, and flu-like symptoms were all possible if we went too hard too fast. Thus, this was going to be an extremely slow process. We needed to test Ava's body carefully to see what it could handle and adjust as needed. The practitioner said her body would slowly give us cues as to when we could push just a little more.

I started taking her for massages more regularly, including one called a craniosacral massage, which is a hands-on technique. It uses gentle touch to help calm the nervous system, and it's hands down Ava's favorite. She started doing occasional magnesium salt water floats, chiropractic care, sauna, and cold plunges. I attended every single visit with her; she was too weak and unstable to do them alone. She was seventeen at this time, and we hadn't even given drivers education a thought.

I would sit in dark, hot rooms peeling layers of clothes off, feeling like I was literally sucking on a hairdryer while she floated naked in the salt water. I would catch up on my emails, sometimes down to just my bra, while pouring sweat, listening to the sweet sounds of Ava's snores as she floated peacefully. I would have given anything to make the comfort of that last longer than the sixty minutes it took to complete. I would hold her hand as she went back and forth between a hot sauna and a cold plunge. I helped her up each step one at a time, like an elderly grandma, until she could little by little lower her body into the freezing water.

She was extremely heat intolerant at this point and was still feeling lightheaded often, so we wanted to start out slow in the sauna with just a few minutes at a time. After much thought, and the time involved in all of these healing modalities, I decided it would be worth the investment to purchase an in-home sauna and red light therapy machine for her to use at her disposal under my watch.

It took nearly three months for the first drop of sweat to appear. By this point, she had worked up to approximately twenty-minute sessions three to four times per week. I'll never forget her screaming for me—I came running in a panic. I opened the sauna door and saw a huge smile on her face. "MOM, LOOK!" she yelled, pointing to her forehead where I saw three tiny little drops of sweat. I honestly don't think I have ever been that excited in my life! I jumped up and down like a little kid on Christmas. Every drop of sweat was a drop of poison coming out of her body.

By this time, we had moved back into our home. It only took a week, but it felt like a year. The remediation was complete: the ducts had been cleaned, the entire house had been fogged with Decon 30, and a UV-C light for coil disinfection was now installed above our HVAC unit, which meant every particle of air that came into our ducts had to pass by that light first. If there was anything harmful in the air, it would be killed before entering the ducts and dispersed into our home. I had also purchased an Air Oasis purifier for her bedroom that used five technologies to attack and remove mold, mold spores, mycotoxins, and beta-glucans. The kids were all still rooming together while we waited for the contractors to finish putting back and replacing all that was ripped out during remediation. To this day, Ava has not had a single nosebleed since reentering our home.

We increased the binders by just a touch, and her body reminded us yet again how riddled with toxins it was. Her pathways were not yet working sufficiently and she experienced her first of many Herxheimer reactions. She missed school more than she went those days, and I had stopped caring. Her school counselor was wonderful during this time and extremely accommodating. Ava would lie there, her mattress on the floor of our office and workout room, vomiting with a low-grade fever and flu-like symptoms. It was pathetic to watch, but it was different this time—we finally had answers and a reason for it all. Ava knew that this awful feeling was the poisons literally being pulled from her body, and this knowledge made it a little easier for her to bear.

It was a few months later before we were able to allow the children to return to their fully redone rooms, which we say now have the cleanest air on Earth! Though the remediation was complete, that didn't mean anything was put back together. The team had removed the mold, ripped out carpets and windows, and helped removed the heavy mattresses and furniture, but we still had to hire contractors to put everything back together, shop to replace items, and wait while the work was done. The kids were all beyond delighted and very ready at that point to have their own spaces again. Ava was finally able to pick up Wasabi from his extended stay at the bird hotel, which he had stayed nearly three months at, and settle into her new room. I could tell that even though she was still extremely sick, she could breathe at last.

It's funny how the world has shaped us, without our knowledge or consent to what we believe, and the severity of life's obstacles. Don't get me wrong, we have many people in our lives that care deeply and understood the magnitude of the situation we were dealing with, but many did not. If you have a house fire, people swoop in to help. Strangers donate money, and people come out of the woodwork to offer their services. The financial burden may not be there due to insurance typically covering that sort of thing, but even strangers tend to weep for the sentimental things that were lost and the trauma of it all. There are certain things that generate automatic empathy and certain things that don't. I can tell you that having mold in your home, and mold toxicity in your child, do not bear the same heaviness, concern, or credibility. I started asking myself why that is.

As Ava was slowly beginning to heal without the use of additional pharmaceuticals, all of the dots in my life started connecting. Most everything she was using to heal, God had provided in some way on this Earth for the purpose of restoring health or curing disease. In Genesis 1:29–31, God said, "Behold, I have given you every plant yielding seed that is on the fence of all the earth, and every tree with seed in its fruit. You shall have them for food. And to every beast of the earth and to every bird of the heavens and to everything that creeps on the earth, everything that has the breath of life, I have given every green plant for food."

The herbs, supplements, and whole foods in their natural form all derived from nature, not a lab. Even the sauna, although much upgraded from the Native American traditions of the sweat lodge, served many of the same purposes. Hot stones placed in the center with herbs and water was a sacred place for healing during a journey of physical, emotional, or spiritual cleansing.

I thought back to an appointment we had at the hospital with a nutritionist after Ava's ulcerative colitis diagnosis. It had been the biggest waste of time. Even Ava, who was just fifteen at the time, immediately spewed her disgust for the nutrition advice this woman gave her. Diet never seemed to come up in the discussions as something that would make a positive difference; the focus was always on a lab test or a prescription drug. Their attention would only spike when I mentioned something that was considered naturopathic or holistic in nature. Their perplexed facial expressions usually led me to believe that they disapproved, or were too proud to admit they were uneducated in that area. I began to wonder why the medical community didn't typically recognize environmental illnesses and why they certainly didn't use anything outside the box of Big Pharma to treat it. I thought about all the years I had blindly trusted that these doctors knew best. Little did I know that there was a whole world of natural treatments that could not only heal, but that also didn't have a list of side effects a mile long.

The pharmaceutical industry pours money into medical schools to create connections. Payments to physicians are common, and it makes me wonder how money influences physicians' prescribing tendencies and behavior. I've often thought about how the pharmaceutical companies might have influenced the curriculum in medical schools. Then I began to wonder about these similarities in our public school systems as well, and how the agendas of our government and the powerful people and companies of our world slowly trickle down to infiltrate our schools and the minds of our children. Are these doctors and educators actually being brainwashed and molded this way on purpose? To become pawns used to generate the most money possible for Big Pharma once they are practicing? To perhaps corrupt the minds of our youth, deviously creating a future unlike anything we have ever known to serve their covetous greed?

You only know what you are taught or what you seek to learn for yourself. Certain conditions and healing modalities seem to be purposely left out of the curriculum for a very calculated reason. If you never have an adverse event in your life that drives you to think outside the box—a passion so deep, it pushes through everything you once thought to be the truth—then you may never realize that you have become a puppet in the game of greed and power.

I think I now know the reason for all of this, and it sickens me. The FDA doesn't approve the in-depth testing needed for many of these types of environmental illnesses, and doctors are only trained to treat very specific things and are given particular courses of action that are approved up the chain of command.

Things like saunas, supplements, herbs, whole foods grown from the earth without pesticides, and a nontoxic lifestyle would never make Big Pharma any money. Finding the root cause of a child's gender dysphoria wouldn't generate the need for expensive surgeries and life-altering drugs. Holding off on any puberty blockers or hormones until they have a fully developed brain wouldn't force these innocent children to be tethered to

Big Pharma for life and generate a confirmed stream of income. Have you ever paid attention to the stories of detransitioners? Probably not, because they are cast aside and not given a platform. Their stories of awakening to regret are suffocated because it doesn't fit into the narrative the rulers of the world are pushing.

If these complex illnesses were recognized in conventional medicine and treated more holistically, insurance companies would have to foot the bill for these treatments. It's all connected, and it seems to be driven by egotistical, greedy companies and their insatiable desire for wealth and power.

I can understand how a trained mind can be almost impossible to change. But when you see something happen before your own eyes, you have to accept a new reality, one that opens your mind and your heart to a world you previously didn't know existed.

Watching Ava's symptoms start to dissipate was truly like watching a miracle unfold. You really had to see it with your own eyes to believe it. Slowly, I saw her energy increase, and I noticed she wasn't sleeping as much during the day. I started to realize it had been a while since I heard her complain of a racing heart or feeling lightheaded. Her appetite had increased slightly; her eyes looked just a little bit more alive. It was happening very slowly, but I knew I was starting to see something extraordinary unfold.

I don't have many witnesses who saw Ava often enough for it to impact their belief system. Ava was picky about who she would emerge from her bedroom for besides family. But the lives of the few who were able to watch this undeniable transformation will forever be changed.

My sister, of course—who is now seeking out functional medicine for her own family—has been forever altered. Roxanne, who observed Ava regularly, has told me that she will never look at her patients in the same way ever again. She's expressed that if she were younger, just starting out in her career, that the miracle she witnessed in Ava would have changed the course of her life, perhaps even calling her to the field of functional medicine.

This is a woman who has spent years in conventional medicine. She questioned me often, spending time away from her own family to listen to me ramble on and on and on about my theories. She's an extremely intelligent woman who wanted answers as much as I did. She pushed back as much as she possibly could, questioning, skeptical, and leaning on her years of schooling and training, but here she saw something that defied everything she had been taught. She watched me desperately seeking answers, holding reservations yet being optimistic at the same time. Time after time, she witnessed my gut instincts being right. She saw in real time, with her own eyes, Ava slowly starting to come back to life. She saw something she cannot unsee and is now, too, a believer.

Healing God's way, as I now like to refer to it, was also witnessed by my friend Adriane. She is the kind of friend your soul connects with and you just know you were intertwined in a former life somehow. Our families grew closer as our boys discovered the love of baseball together. Between the chaos of six kids combined, multiple sports, jobs, and extracurricular activities, and the love of watching our boys on the baseball diamond, a special friendship was born. This is a woman who shed tears watching Ava's senior photoshoot. She had invested time not just into Vinny because he was buddies with her son, but the girls as well.

By this time, Ava was well into her senior year of high school. The last year of high school had somehow still arrived amongst the dumpster fire of the last few years. I had actually done all the paperwork to pull her from in-person school and allow her to finish high school online. With as much school as she had missed the year prior along with the endless appointments and the intense protocol she was following, I just didn't see how traditional school would fit in.

Her entire high school career had been nothing but Covid and sickness. She hadn't been able to experience the things she should have. She wasn't there enough and was too sick to create lasting friendships, go to parties or dances, or learn to drive. Even the thought of college, which I had always made a priority, had not been discussed. I thought, if anything, maybe she would take a few classes at the community college a few miles down the road.

But as summer came to an end, things were looking up enough to convince her to try to finish high school in person. Being a senior allowed her to start later, along with having a few fun art classes she had earned by getting the tougher ones out of the way years prior. I still drove her and picked her up every day. I would pull up to the school daily, unload her wheelchair, and watch her roll in, just praying that my efforts would prove fruitful.

At this point, the botched chop job she had done on her hair had started growing out. I had used my cosmetology skills to slowly start removing the black box color she had ruined her natural locks with, and she was slowly beginning to resemble the girl I once knew.

When Ava came to me and showed interest in having senior pictures done, I was honestly shocked. For starters, I hadn't thought that would be something she wanted to do, nor something I thought she would have the energy or confidence for. Then she laid out her request, and it was a big one: She explained that it was her wish to have her senior pictures done with the jet her father flew. The closest base that housed those jets was in Virginia. I wasn't sure I even had the connections for a request like that, nor did I think she was in any shape to travel. But I had to at least give it a shot.

To my complete and utter shock, it turned out the jets were going to be downtown from us just two weeks later for an airshow! So, Jeff's old squadron commander and his wife went to work for Ava and made it happen. I scrambled to look for a photographer, and it just so happened that the one who had done a shoot for the girls years prior, for a non-profit called Project: Model for a Day, was available and willing.

We had met him during this wonderful experience designed to give young women going through tough medical obstacles the opportunity to become a supermodel for a day. I will forever be grateful for the memories, pictures, and experience of that day, and the best part now was that he was already fully aware of our backstory. It felt like it was meant to be that he truly understood the significance behind what he was about to capture for us. We were able to meet the jets in a private area without any crowds of people. The red carpets were laid out, and the girls felt like celebrities.

Adriane had offered to go as our assistant to help with whatever was needed, and the girls were happy to have her with them. She had prior experience being an assistant, and she definitely shined as she rushed in with bags of clothes, Christian Louboutin pumps, makeup, and anything and everything else the girls could have possibly needed. I had nothing but my purse and my phone, and this was part of the reason we made a good team! Adriane should have been an assistant to the stars—she was that good. She catered to their every possible need and made them feel so important and loved.

Stella, of course, also wanted in on some photos, as this was a once-in-a-lifetime opportunity, so we decided to combine Ava's senior pictures with some of the girls together in honor of their dad. It was bittersweet for me. I knew I could never look at that jet again with the wonder, awe, and pride in my heart I used to feel when I saw it fly. To me, it would always be the machine that hadn't been good enough to save my husband's life.

Imagine going to a prison and confronting the murderer of your loved one as you look them in the eye. That is what I felt like I was about to do as we drove there. As we entered the building and were led out to the tarmac, I had flashes of our previous life and remembered that the girls didn't have many, if any, memories of this life. They had been far too young. To them, they were experiencing watching this supersonic jet come in for a landing for the very first time.

As I watched them standing there—exchanging silent glances, eyes to the sky, watching this magnificent machine come in to land—I realized that this moment was for them. It wasn't about me at all. I needed to push my own feelings and memories to the side and soak in the pride they felt for their father during that moment. It's different to see something for yourself, with your own eyes.

They had long forgotten their days as babies and toddlers, running through the squadron bar and around the jets parked in the hangar. I can still vividly remember the days when Ava would stuff a Polly Pocket or her tiny Blueberry Muffin doll, which had belonged to my sister as a child and still smelled exactly the same, into one of the pockets of her father's flight suit. "My baby wants a jet ride today, Daddy," she would say. He would smile, give her a hug, and walk out the door to work, and she would patiently wait to hear the tale of all the things her babies had seen on their adventures.

Stella has no recollection of meeting Santa for the very first time in an airplane hangar, or her dad chuckling at her hesitation to be placed in his lap and comforting her with a hug and kiss. The girls had forgotten the life they lived, thinking that Daddy working alert during the holidays might mean he actually got to help Santa deliver presents if he was in a pinch.

They don't remember the many times they spent standing on the tarmac feeling the roar of their dad's passion in their chest as his jet soared above the clouds, or running to him as he climbed down the ladder after a deployment or TDY. Up until now, they only remembered the stories

I had told them or pictures I had shown them. This time was different. They were experiencing a piece of something that their dad had loved as young intelligent women who were fully able to grasp all it entailed. They felt connected to him in a way they had never before. As I looked over at Adriane, she had tears streaming down her face.

I was finally able to feel thankful at that moment as I stared at something that, for a long time, had only represented death. Watching it breathe a piece of their dad's life back into them mended a part of me that no longer needed to remain broken. I found gratitude watching the girls have this unforgettable moment, intertwined with pride, sadness, loss, and admiration.

By this point, Ava was in school pretty regularly. The calls from the nurse had stopped, as well as her constant texts informing me of yet another bloody nose, racing heart, or ailment. We had been seeing her practitioner long enough to start repeating some of her labs. Not only was she feeling better, but her labs proved that her protocol was working. Her inflammatory markers were lowering, her body being replenished of what had been depleted, and her gut was healing. Her calprotectin level was even down to seventeen, which is unheard of for someone with IBD. As her body slowly released the poisons, it was finally able to start healing.

At school, she was not only completing all her schoolwork on time— she was getting fantastic grades! Ava had always struggled in math and hadn't been without a tutor since middle school, and even with the extra help, she often still struggled to maintain a C average. This year, her senior year, was the first time ever she didn't have a tutor for math. To this very day, she has not received below an A- on any math assignment or test.

We laughed when I jokingly asked her if she was cheating. Ava told me that all of a sudden, she just understood. She wasn't studying extra because she didn't need to; she said she was able to focus in class and comprehend everything immediately, and it felt easy. She said her brain felt like it had been scrubbed clean. The only things that had changed were removing her from a toxic environment and implementing the necessary things to detox. In my opinion, you don't "all of a sudden" become a wiz at math when you're seventeen after years of barely passing.

That really made me wonder how long these toxins had been hurting her—and at what depth they had affected her before it was significant enough to force me to research. I realized the genetic factors involved had been there from birth and always would be. But what about the rest of it? Were these all legitimate diagnoses, or were they the results of the accumulation of toxins building up over time? I started to wonder if every illness diagnosed that didn't have a definitive diagnostic test could be potentially due to toxic overload. And what about autoimmune diseases? Doctors claim they are a mystery, but are they really?

I thought about the less significant things that were considered common in childhood with my other children and wondered if they could have been avoided had our home been healthy, our food not riddled with poisons, and their bodies not injected with so many vaccines as babies.

I know that many of us don't have the genetic makeup or a compromised immune system that makes it hard to detox, but that doesn't mean these things were not affecting us in a negative way. I think about how Stella and Vinny both had chronic croup when they were little to the point that their tonsils finally had to be removed, as they would get so swollen, we worried about their airway closing. I thought about my constant allergies and Vinny's skin sensitivities, ADHD, behavioral issues, eczema, asthma, ulcerative colitis, and C-diff. I thought about all of it, big and small, and I couldn't shake thinking that perhaps it was all connected. I guess I may never know, but I will always wonder, and I will never stop digging for the truth.

The only thing I could do now was keep pushing forward, spreading awareness, and speaking my mind and pushing the boundaries of everything I had been taught to believe in hopes of awakening more hearts and minds with our story.

With every passing week, it seemed Ava was improving in small ways. Almost all of her symptoms had dissipated or at least decreased significantly, except her legs. She was still having bilateral leg pain, her feet were still numb, and her right foot was still dragging. Her functional medicine practitioner prescribed something called LDN, low-dose naltrexone. I had heard of naltrexone, which is FDA approved for both opioid and alcohol use disorders, but I had never heard of LDN.

LDN is used for chronic pain, is anti-inflammatory, and can help manage anxiety and depression. It is inexpensive to make, has been around for a very long time, and has a very good safety profile. So, why had I never heard of this before? Why wouldn't Ava have been offered this prior to starting the pharmaceuticals she was prescribed for ulcerative colitis and anxiety that had some pretty hefty side effects? Turns out that conventional medicine doesn't use this drug, at all. We had to have it compounded at a functional medicine pharmacy. As Ava slowly works her way up to the therapeutic dose, our hope is eventually to eliminate every other pharmaceutical and have LDN be the only thing she takes.

Eventually, she was able to walk slowly around the house but still used a walker out and about and a wheelchair at school. That was the only way possible for her to make it to all her classes on time; it still took her a good ten minutes to walk from the driveway to the house after getting out of the car. I was so happy and relieved that everything seemed to be moving in the right direction but very concerned that there had been zero improvement in her legs. I kept telling myself that maybe, because this was the first symptom to appear, it would be the last to see any improvements. But something inside me stirred again with that old familiar feeling.

What if there was something else going on? What if there was another part of this complex puzzle that we had yet to discover? I couldn't help myself, and so I started to conduct my next investigation.

Ava's practitioner knew my concerns, and we decided to go ahead and order another set of tests we had talked about in the beginning but hadn't yet done. Ava had been so sick when we started working with her, and it doesn't always make sense to run every test imaginable right out of the gate. You start with the biggest areas of concern, and as you peel back each layer of the onion, you work on one thing at a time. That is one of the biggest problems people have when they start trying to heal themselves from complex illnesses—they try to do it all at once, overwhelm their body, and end up so miserable, they give up.

We completed the testing, and now it was time to wait. I didn't even question my gut instincts anymore. I considered them a superpower and welcomed whatever they might be leading me to. I wasn't afraid of what I would find; I was only fearful of not being able to find what I was looking for.

CHAPTER 12
TICK, TICK BOOM?

I was never interested in politics as a child. I actually found it quite dull, even as a young adult. It never seemed like it would have that big of an effect on my life, no matter what happened or who got elected, and I certainly never felt like I could make a change. So, I just chose to not really think about it. To me, politics were something monotonous that old people talked about at the dinner table. My dad was a colonel in the Army, so the only thing that had ever piqued my interest was our military and keeping them safe. Other than that, I just didn't understand any of it. I was one of those naive people who didn't think anything I did could ever help make the world a better place, so instead I just focused on making my world a fun place to be.

When my children were young, it seemed more and more kids were becoming vocal about politics. It's not that they actually understood any of it, though; they would just spew back whatever their parents said. I remember a confrontation my nephew once had on the bus when another boy threatened to hurt him if his dad voted for the "wrong" guy in the upcoming election. It was then I decided I wouldn't talk to my kids about my personal affiliation or chosen candidate. Instead, I taught them to research everything.

I would explain that at their age, it was more important to learn about all sides of the government and what they represent, rather than potentially having political arguments on a grade school bus over something they didn't understand. Part of me still believes that, but I also never thought our world would look the way it does today. I wish I would have had deeper conversations with them when they were younger on these topics. I think if I had done that, I wouldn't be trying so hard now to make up for lost time in a world that is headed in the wrong direction. But if they are anything like me—and they are—they will have an event in their life that sparks an interest, and they will figure it out in their own way, on their own terms.

If I had to go back in time and have a conversation with my younger self about my worldly views and beliefs, I would probably smack my ignorant self right across the face. I had grown up with a strong set of morals instilled in me early by my parents, but I was also easily influenced by trends, celebrities, and whatever was popular at that moment in time. But hey, that's why there are rules set in place—such as age of consent and parental rights—to help us be protected during our years of emotional immaturity, bad choices, raging hormones, and thinking you know everything about life.

Back when I was a kid, those things actually mattered. We may not have liked authority, but the fear of it kept us in line, and communication between parents and the other adults helping to shape us seemed to align for a common purpose. Kids were kids, and the general consensus was to keep parents informed and in charge. In today's world, it feels like those things are actively challenged and almost intentionally removed. It feels more and more that we live in a world where our children and their underdeveloped brains are allowed more power over their choices than their own parents. It seems more than just mainstream media has turned into something completely driven by outside connections, financial gains, and political agendas. I continue to tell my children to never blindly believe what they hear on the news, in a doctor's office, in a classroom, or online.

When did it become almost impossible to figure out the truth? Everything has somehow turned political. And now it was directly affecting me and my family, which made it personal.

I finally realized that the changes do start with people like me. Think about the people in your life who are the best at what they do—the best doctors, teachers, parents, etc. They are all people who have experienced some type of monumental event in their life that created desire and passion. Passion, whether joyful or driven by anger or sadness, creates empathy and drive. It creates the motivation to start making noise. Noise wakes people up, brings attention. The true change takes place when the attention something gets becomes so loud that it is impossible to ignore.

"I think Ava has Lyme disease," I blurted out to Roxanne over a glass of wine.

"What the F!!" she said with wide eyes. "Why do you think that?"

I had been thinking about Ava's childhood a lot while I cared for her during these past few years, probably because many of the things I had been doing for her were the same things I did for her as an infant and toddler. Bathing her, holding her, making sure she was fed, advocating for her, protecting her from germs just like a newborn baby with an underdeveloped immune system. She was fragile, weak, and incapable of caring for herself. It was my job to keep her alive.

Our backyard had a huge river of rocks in it when we first moved in. It snaked back and forth and went underneath a tiny white bridge surrounded by bushes and a garden. We called it the Rocky River, and the girls called the white bridge the Troll Bridge. It made me happy to see them running outside, free and happy. It took some getting used to not to be on the lookout for a bear or a moose to wander into the yard.

I hadn't yet fenced in the yard, and I needed things to occupy them. Being a single mom was a lot of work. I prided myself on coming up with fun things to entertain them while I got things done. As one example, I would buy huge tubs of paint and brushes and tell them to make the Rocky River beautiful. Stella would always paint a few rocks here and there and be on to the next thing, but not Ava. She would sit in the grass and move slowly along the rocks, sometimes painting for hours. And she only used blue—always blue.

Blue has always been her favorite color. Ava's preschool teacher in Alaska had always purchased extra blue paint just for her; she joked years later that she still had a supply left from Ava's time there. As a child, Ava had been mesmerized by the blue morpho butterfly. Her dad had purchased a fake plastic one for her as a child, and they used to hide it around the house for each other to find. I believe she still has it to this day. She always says if she ever gets a tattoo, it will probably be the blue morpho butterfly.

One day, after a round of painting, she came inside to show me a mark on her leg. It was a single red circle, darker on the outside like a bullseye. She said it didn't bother her. I had her take a shower and I put some hydrocortisone cream on it, and I told her we would keep a close eye on it. The next morning, it was still there, and after looking up pictures to see if I could properly identify it, I thought that perhaps it could be a tick bite. We soon went to the doctor to have it checked out and I asked specifically if he thought that is what it could be. He immediately shook his head no, told me it should go away with the cream, and to call back if she developed any symptoms.

It did go away, and she didn't develop any symptoms. Within a few days, we had forgotten all about it. I go back to that moment often and wish I would have pushed to have her tested, but I had been uninformed—and that should have been his job, not mine.

I kept seeing the mold and Lyme combo brought up in the groups I had started joining on social media. It seemed as though they went hand in hand often, and that led me down a path to figure out why that was. I learned that the classic Lyme rash, called "expanding erythema migrans," actually only appears in less than fifty percent of Lyme cases. I also learned that you can be bitten by an infected tick and not have any symptoms in the moment; it can lie dormant in your body, just waiting for something to trigger it to come to life. Mold is one of the things that can trigger it.

Mold toxicity can cause people to develop symptoms from Lyme disease, and Lyme infections can cause symptoms from mold. If the body's immune system is working properly, it removes biotoxins on its own and the person will remain symptom-free. For those with Lyme, however, the body is already compromised and in a weakened state, unable to keep up with the breakdown of toxins efficiently, which causes the toxic bucket to fill and overflow. Everyone is born with a bucket. Your genetic makeup and environment will determine how fast it will fill with toxins. When it starts to spill over and your body can't detox fast enough is when issues begin to make themselves known.

Lyme disease is a mimicking illness, similar to mold. Its symptoms can include but are not limited to migraines, headaches, POTS, dizziness, brain fog, cognitive dysfunction, neuropathy, numbing, tingling, ataxia, and joint and bone pain, and it has been known to be misdiagnosed as multiple sclerosis and many other things.

Roxanne had stopped questioning me like she had in the past. "I don't want to believe it because it sounds crazy," she said. "But with your track record, I wouldn't be surprised if you are right."

Turns out, I was right. But in the true fashion of our life, there would still be a surprise: Ava tested positive for not just one, but two strains of Lyme—Borrelia burgdorferi and Borrelia afzelii. The odd thing is that the first one is native to North America, while the second is the most common cause of Lyme disease in Europe. We had taken a family trip to Europe when Ava was nine years old. This was just mind-blowing to me.

She also tested positive for Epstein-Barr virus and eight different heavy metals. Arsenic, beryllium, gadolinium, tellurium, thorium, tungsten, barium, and bismuth were all found in her body, the highest of those being beryllium, gadolinium, and thorium. The scariest thing about seeing these results was knowing that many of them wouldn't have even registered as a positive according to the CDC and the tests that would be administered from a conventional doctor.

This brings me to the reasons I believe Lyme disease and other environmental illnesses are not always tested properly, and the reason behind these horrific complex illnesses that have created such a political divide. Proper treatment and diagnostics should be available for every person, without the massive financial burden. The thought that politics could have somehow prevented my daughter from getting well enraged me.

The treatment approach when it comes to Lyme is definitely not a bipartisan one. The IDSA (Infectious Diseases Society of America) and the ILADS (International Lyme and Associated Diseases Society) do not have the same guidelines for treatment. Only the ILADS provides care for persistent or chronic Lyme patients, and this care is not covered by insurance, which prevents many from getting the care that they need and deserve. The testing done by the IDSA only looks for antibodies, not the actual bacteria itself, and can easily result in a false negative. If you research who is responsible for writing the guidelines for the IDSA, it is interesting to see the connections they have to insurance and pharmaceutical companies.

Again, we were faced with something incredibly odd, highly controversial, and politically driven. The universe was speaking to me in a way I couldn't ignore anymore.

Throughout the course of our journey and the many awakenings I had experienced, I decided to start asking questions about how my children's schools were handling all the changes that were happening at what seemed to be a rapid pace. I had heard stories of kids identifying as cats and dogs, referring to themselves as "furries." Schools using certain pronouns for students or treating them as specific gender identities at school and then using different ones when calling home to parents started popping up on my news sites. Boys identifying as girls being allowed in the women's bathrooms and pornographic books being distributed in the school library, and sometimes even used as part of a school's curriculum, seemed like situations that were beginning to be normalized.

So, I decided I would stop wondering and start asking questions. The biggest problem I was having with all this was the trend of secrecy. The slow transfer of parental rights to teachers, medical professionals, social workers, and therapists without permission seemed to be happening under the radar. Since when were parents left in the dark on purpose? None of this sounded okay to me, so I set out to find out if any of these things were happening at my own children's schools without my knowledge.

I wanted to be an informed parent, and I definitely wanted to be the first to discuss such topics if needed with my children before it was presented to them by someone else. My internal drive to protect them and exert my parental rights to be informed was in high gear.

As I began my new quest to uncover any secret agendas at the schools, I was also preparing for Ava to start a new treatment protocol. Unfortunately, Ava's practitioner did not treat Lyme disease. After the little research I had done, it wasn't hard to understand why. This meant a brand-new doctor, who also didn't take insurance and could be quite expensive, had to be found.

The thought of integrating the protocols of two different practitioners overwhelmed me a little. Fortunately, Ava's current practitioner had a recommended Lyme-literate practitioner for us, which saved me time and allowed me to feel comfortable that she could be trusted. Thankfully, she was on the list of suggested providers by the Global Lyme Alliance. "Lyme literate" means that the practitioner is extremely familiar with the vast range of symptoms involved, as well as secondary issues, coinfections, and the difficulty generally involved in treating a complex illness.

We had a few treatment options to choose from regarding coinfections, such as Doxycycline, Methylene blue, Disulfiram, and Alinia. We planned to start some antivirals for the Epstein-Barr virus, which included two natural remedies called Cryptolepis sanguinolenta and Japanese knotweed, and also olive leaf extract. The roots of Cryptolepis are traditionally used in West Africa for malaria but have also been shown to support Lyme based on the herb's antibacterial and anti-inflammatory properties. The use of a Japanese knotweed tincture has been known to help combat bacteria produced by a Lyme infection. Its plant extract is powerful and has many benefits. Olive leaf extract promotes the body's ability to fight viruses and can inhibit and break down biofilm formation.

Biofilm is a slimy toxic substance that can form around bacteria, making it extremely difficult for an antibiotic or medicine to penetrate and kill those organisms. Biofilms protect these bacteria in the body and allow them to thrive. In order to properly kill the bacteria, the biofilms must be broken down or eliminated for the chosen method of treatment to begin working. I was not well versed in Lyme at all at this point; I was following my gut instincts and felt good about the professionals we were working with. Given the dramatic improvements we had seen taking a more natural route, Ava and I were on board to give this a shot.

Even though Ava was still using her wheelchair, and we didn't yet know if any of this pain or damage would be permanent, we started discussing the possibility of her attending college the next year. As she started to heal, I think we both felt that this could potentially be a real option. It wouldn't be easy—and it would certainly be frightening for me to send her out of our clean bubble of healing—but I was desperate for her to spread her wings and gain the confidence she would need to realize how capable she is and to start living her life. I needed her to know that she was far more than the bad things in life that had happened to her. She was not a diagnosis, illness, or a traumatic event. Those things do not define her.

We decided to do a few college visits, with no pressure, to see what she thought. And we did just that. Our list of questions to ask were not typical of what you would expect of a senior in high school. Ava wanted to know about accessibility—if she would be able to easily get around if she were still in a wheelchair, if the cafeteria had any food options she could eat, if any of the dorms she would possibly be living in had water damage or were old construction. These would be things that she would forever question. It had become a part of her life, and all of ours. It would be crucial for her to take the best care of herself possible as she ventured out into the world, whether that be the air she breathes, the food she nourishes her body with, or the products she uses for self-care and cleaning. It would all matter immensely.

She had become very dependent on me over the years, though for good reason and no fault of her own. This was a battle no one should have to fight alone, nor could they possibly do so while in the depths of its wrath. I knew she would eventually have to be on her own and wouldn't fully gain the confidence to know she could do it by herself until she didn't have me in the next room, or even the next town.

We visited a small beautiful university a little over an hour away. It was big enough to seem exciting to her, yet small enough to keep her anxiety away, and close enough to home if she needed me. It was accommodating in every way, and the cafeteria did not disappoint. I didn't put any pressure on her, as I knew we still had a long road ahead, but I told her to think about it, research more on her own, and keep it in mind as we planned a few more visits to other schools.

I remembered all the times I had reminded my kids that there is always a silver lining to anything bad, no matter how horrific. Sometimes it takes years to figure out what it is. But the days will continue to come and go and, if you're looking hard enough, you will find a lesson or reason within them. Their dad always used to say that people are put on this Earth for one of two reasons: to teach a lesson, or to be taught one. Perhaps Ava was meant for both.

"I'm going to submit my application, Mom," she said. She was worried about her grade point average—due to what had transpired the year prior, I'm sure you can imagine why. Her entire high school career had been riddled with illness. She had managed to maintain good grades, but this time was different. She knew her junior year would lower her four-year GPA and could negatively affect a college acceptance decision. "I am going to write an amazing essay and hope for the best," she said matter-of-factly. She looked up at me, her blue eyes now looking bright, her healing now starting to show in her fresh pale skin, and added with confidence, "I want to study toxicology. If I get accepted, that will be my major."

She explained to me her obvious interest, how her story, background, and personal hardships in life could create some real change and make a difference somehow—she could feel it. And with that one simple sentence, my heart filled with pride, because I knew. She had discovered her moment in time, the thing that wakes you up enough to have the desire, the determination, and the noise loud enough to go out into the world not only to make a name for yourself, but to change the lives of others while doing it.

CHAPTER 13
MORE THAN JUST A BOOK

Want your son to learn about eating pussy? How about a book with cartoons of children performing oral sex for your child's enjoyment? Or perhaps you'd like your child to check out a guidebook that teaches them how to bind their breasts or pack a penis to begin their social gender transition? I'm sure most of you have no idea what I'm talking about, but your child could be learning about these very things every day at many schools across the country. When they walk out the door into the place you've entrusted to teach them, have you ever researched what they are actually being educated about? Were you aware that all these things—and more, probably—reside in your child's public school library, just waiting for them to check out, totally unbeknownst to you?

Digging deeper into the public school system was astonishing. There are plenty of things I absolutely love about the school my children attended. The accommodations for special needs are beyond stellar; I have always been impressed and happy with how that aspect has been handled. Whether it was something as simple as speech therapy or more in-depth things, as had become necessary with Ava, they were always extremely well taken care of and set up for success. Along the way, my children have had many wonderful teachers and educators who truly helped to shape them in positive ways. These were the kinds of people who entered the profession for all the right reasons. Some of them, I even became personal friends with. They were phenomenal teachers and humans who often went out of their way for my children and many others.

As time goes by, this also seems to feel like a thing of the past. There are many educators now, as things trickle down the chain of command, who have decided to bring their political agendas and personal beliefs into the classroom. For some reason, they feel it is their right to fill the heads of children with ideologies and to normalize the sexualization of minors, all under the umbrella of education and the creation of global citizens.

The drive to remain neutral, not ruffle any feathers, and hide behind the cloak of inclusivity has slowly allowed feelings to become more important than facts. The fear of exerting authority and having the guts to actually take a stance on controversial subjects has allowed things like kitty litter boxes to be considered necessary in the school restrooms for those students who identify as furries.

But I actually think the biggest problem is the people who are not aware this is happening. I still believe there is more good in this world than evil; I just think the world has gotten turned upside down and people are just extremely unaware. Situational awareness has gone out the window as people stare at their phones, and it allows destruction to creep in unnoticed.

As I began to ask questions and became educated on the laws and guidelines followed at my children's schools, I realized that many times, they didn't always line up with what was actually happening. And most parents, including some staff members, had absolutely no clue what was happening inside the buildings their children attended. I would have been one of these clueless people myself had it not been for my past experiences. My past has made me hypervigilant in all areas of my life, especially when it comes to my children.

I was starting to get the idea that maybe there needed to be some greater awareness on this issue. A gathering to discuss the rapid changes and social contagions happening, and to set firm boundaries on what would be standard practice.

When I discovered a few things that made me uncomfortable, I wanted to bring them to their attention. It may have seemed like something small in the grand scheme of issues that arise when it comes to managing thousands of teenagers, but to me it was not small. It was actually quite large—I just needed a way to explain the bigger picture. I have a hard time thinking anyone would do something that could be damaging to a child on purpose. I am truly a person who wants to get to the bottom of things and educate others properly on a viewpoint that could open their eyes to something questionable they could be doing without awareness. It's when they have gained awareness and the issues are not resolved that a true problem arises.

After all Ava had been through, I was extremely protective of her. I knew she was still in a very vulnerable state. I would get anxiety over things like finding out her school social worker had met with her to discuss her illness during the remediation of our home. I hoped it stemmed from somewhere loving and kind, but it bothered me so deeply that I wasn't asked ahead of time or filled in on what was discussed.

The last thing I needed was another authority figure thinking they had any right to counsel my daughter on things they didn't understand behind my back. None of these people would be a part of her life after she left that building, but the impact they made, big or small, was similar to a person's toxic bucket. One by one, little by little, it fills and eventually spills over and becomes a part of them. She had experienced so much negativity and harmful counseling and I was fiercely protective, as she was still so easy to influence.

And again, the trend of secrecy, the removal of parent involvement, and the infiltration of someone I didn't know thinking she had authority over my child gave me immense stress and uneasy feelings. I didn't have a way at the time to explain why that was. I simply vowed to find a way to bring this to light for the many unknowing parents who I knew had not a clue.

My questions seemed to either go unanswered or were met with attempts to smooth them over. I think, for the most part, this was due to lack of proper communication all around. Of course, there are always a few bad apples that ruin it for everyone, but this was a good place with good people, in an intelligent tight-knit community.

It was never my intention to put any school in a bad light, but I had decided it was time to be loud enough to force people to wake up. Unfortunately, this cannot typically be done with a phone call or email. By this point in my life, I was fairly comfortable using my voice to start the noise. I had a reason for every decision I made, every email I sent, and every wrong or complaint I addressed. I decided I would do something loud enough that was impossible to ignore.

I eventually discovered their school housed a plethora of books that were in no way appropriate for minor children. This was not something specific to our school district, but somewhere along the line it had become quite normal across the country. But why was no one talking about this? There was a disconnect, not just in schools but everywhere. Change needed to start small. Something needed to happen to open people's eyes, like mine had been, and inspire them to dig deeper, stay diligent, and continue to be aware of what and who was impacting their children.

I had no issues with the books themselves. I am an avid reader and I believe every story, opinion, lifestyle choice, religion, and race deserves to have their words be available to anyone who could in some way benefit from reading them. I do not, however, believe this is the same for children when it includes adult explicit content. There needs to be a standard, a precedent set for what is deemed appropriate when it comes to minors. It doesn't matter if the Internet allows access to worse things or that the world in general can steal their innocence years earlier than it ever did when I was young.

Kids need the adults in their life to remind them they are children—and to allow them to be. Authority figures need to set strong boundaries and parameters, such as the content used for education in the schools. There will be plenty of time for the evil of this world to tempt them to grow up quicker than they ought to, but adults using this as an excuse is pathetic. But truthfully, I don't think most adults are using this as an excuse; I think they just haven't woken up yet.

When I look back at my childhood, I think the most scandalous thing was maybe looking up the word "penis" in the classroom dictionary and laughing. There was a reason that curtain was in the way back of Blockbuster, you know? Everyone was very aware that what was behind that curtain was not for children. When I was young, the adults in my life all seemed to be on the same page of reality about what was considered appropriate content when it came to kids, especially inside of a school.

My daughter checked out one of the books I described above. It was a good book. It stirred emotions, talked about friendship and love, but it also had pages of extreme and explicit content that was in no way appropriate for a child. And to be frank and surprise you, I honestly would not have had a problem with my daughter reading the particular book she checked out. To me, it was about so much more than just the book.

I have always had an extremely open relationship with all of my children. I have always strived to speak to them about the tough, embarrassing, or controversial things in life years before I think someone else will. It has always been important for me to have the opportunity to do it first, my way. This right is being stripped from parents, and I don't think people are even realizing it because it's happening so slowly. Adults who may not have children's best interests at heart are getting to them first, on purpose, without their parents being aware to guide them. And unfortunately, the good ones that do have their best interests in mind end up getting grouped in with the few that don't.

If we slowly start normalizing this kind of content in schools without anyone speaking up, what happens in the future? I began to question why adult content was now all of a sudden not only allowed and accepted for children, but encouraged. Things had shifted, I was connecting the dots, and it was terrifying.

This was more than just books that would eventually not only be in the library, but in the classroom curriculum. This is how we got to where we are today. People wanting to be indifferent, not wanting to rock the boat, staying silent and letting people live their lives. Most of us just want to be left alone to live our life how we choose, to work for a living, raise a family, have someone to love us, and maybe make a positive difference in the world. And most people don't care how others choose to live theirs—until it starts pressing upon them.

That all started changing when people started demanding other people believe their lies, or their truth, instead of THE truth. Most of the world seemed not to have a clue what was going on, and the ones that did remained silent. This combination seemed to propel the small percentage of people denying objective truth to infect the minds of our youth, and our world. I believe this is happening on purpose, and I felt led to try, in some small way, to make a positive difference.

I decided to attend a board meeting to read out loud some passages from the book that resided in their library that Ava had checked out. I wanted to see how uncomfortable they would be listening to the words that could make even the most uninhibited of a person blush. Most of them appeared to unsuccessfully try to hide their uneasy, awkward, and surprised feelings as I read these words out loud to them. I read loudly, clearly, and slowly and made sure to over-enunciate my words. They more than got my drift, but it's in my nature to be a tad extra! And not one of them seemed to have any clue that this content was readily available for their students.

I was given a complaint form to fill out, and a book review committee was going to be assembled. I was told it would consist of staff and parents with contrary opinions and views. A discussion would be had, and a vote would take place. This would need to be done individually for each and every book that a complaint form was filled out for. The number of people on the committee would need to be odd for voting purposes, yet at the end of it all, the superintendent would be allowed to override the decision. The vote for this particular book did not end in my favor, which was disappointing, yet not all was lost. I had accomplished what I set out to do. My noise was loud enough, and it couldn't be ignored.

I handed the staff eight more complaint forms on my way out the door. I'm sure the thought of having to assemble these meetings and committees, and the time away from their own families it took to do so, was not particularly welcomed. However, in the end, a decision was made to implement a new standard of creating flagged books for adult content and also generating an email to parents each time their child checked out a book in the library. If they could send out an immediate notification when a child's lunch account had a low balance and keep track of tardies and missed assignments easily, they could make this happen, too, without much effort. I don't think this will be an easy task, but it's certainly not a hard one. I think maybe if someone had spoken up prior to me, this would have already been implemented as standard practice.

These changes would, at a minimum, give parents their right to be informed and allow for them to make their own decision on how they wanted to move forward. I suggested a very transparent letter to be sent to parents, along with the changes that would be happening to inform them that this content existed first and foremost, so they would be aware if their child checked out a book with questionable content. They could then exercise their rights as parents however they wished. This was at least the start of putting parents back in the driver's seat.

I didn't get exactly what I wanted, but I did make some noise. Noise that awakened others, and noise that created a change in the right direction.

CHAPTER 14
THE LESSON IN ALL OF IT

Growing up, my mom always used to say that the color purple represented power. I had to be two different people that day many years ago, and on many days throughout my life. What the girls remember as an exciting trip with their aunt to the American Girl store in Chicago was actually a front for me to appear in court regarding the accident that killed their father. I had planned to bring them with me to the courthouse that day just for a short time. "Mommy has a special meeting," I said. "Aunt Kelly is taking you both for a very special day because you are very good girls."

What they may remember as a stop to use the bathroom prior to sending them off on a magical day of fun with their aunt was actually a planned opportunity. For the many there that day, all directly or indirectly connected to their father's death, was an opportunity for them to see, in person, the legacy he had left behind. It was important to me for them to have a real-life image of the sweet, innocent girls who would grow up not knowing their father.

I also needed them to see me as strong and powerful. I know this isn't typically how a widow strives to look or is expected to look. And to many, I'm sure I appeared cold and without emotion. Many would have disagreed with my outward appearance that day, perhaps suggesting that looking timid, sad, and weak would have sparked more empathy.

I needed to look like a bitch that day, a cold-hearted one. I needed to look ice-cold and intimidating. I looked in the mirror, and what I saw staring back was just that. To this day, I think it's perhaps the most confident I have ever looked. A classy, chilling, beautiful, and confident woman was staring back at me, and I felt power in that reflection. If I looked this way, then I could feel this way, too. I needed to feel ice-cold and heartless on that day because I didn't want them to see the actual pain and heartbreak that was alive and thriving on the inside. That part was private, and too much of my privacy and joy had already been stolen without my consent.

I found a deep-purple pencil-skirt dress from J. Crew. The moment I saw it, the color instantly reminded me of power, just as my mother had told me as a child. It was high-necked and sleeveless, but wide over my shoulders. It was a little past knee-length and had a hidden zipper up the back. It was very plain, yet extremely sophisticated, classy, and gorgeous. The instant I saw it, I knew what its purpose would be. I needed to feel all of the things that this dress radiated. Putting it on would be like a costume. If the costume is going to be truly great, you must also encompass the personality and demeanor that makes it come alive. That dress was powerful enough to do just that.

In the rush of getting the girls ready and the hotel room packed, we realized that Snuggie was missing. Stella was completely distraught, and we knew this day would turn into a complete disaster if he wasn't found immediately. On one of the most significant days of my personal life, everything stopped and time stood still. At that moment, there was nothing more important than getting Snuggie back into Stella's arms. Back to the hotel we went to dig through our luggage that had been placed in the back for us until we returned. The fact that I might be late didn't even cross my mind; I was in one hundred percent mom mode.

Walking past a lobby mirror and catching the reflection of a polished shark in a purple power dress caught me off guard. Maybe that was the reason the man behind the desk seemed extremely annoyed at my request to retrieve my luggage yet again; my appearance didn't create much empathy. He probably thought I was headed to a business meeting for some super important company I was running. I looked ruthless, snobby, and arrogant, so he probably thought I was. We all tend to assume things in life, but I have learned not to as much. The world has harshly taught me that lesson. Little did he know, I was just a sad mom in a costume, fighting for my husband's name to be cleared to make sure his death had not been in vain.

No matter what hat I am forced to put on, at the end of the day I will always just be the CEO of my family. It's honestly the most powerful position in the whole world. Snuggie was found wrapped in Stella's pajamas in her suitcase, and instantly all was right in the world again.

We would board a plane that evening, again perhaps not with the exact outcome I had hoped for. But I did create noise, and I definitely forced change. And the girls were filled with gratitude and joy, along with new dolls and matching outfits, and a special memory with their aunt had been created. I left knowing the part I played in bringing awareness and implementing change in their father's jet would save countless lives in the future. I had lost so much, and my girls had lost their father, but I was confident that we had won, too. Our loss was another life saved. There would be families that would never know heartache because of my small voice. It was indeed a victory.

Stella and I recently had a conversation about the feeling you get when someone tells you something is impossible. I told her that many things in life are difficult and challenging, but a strong internal fire can burn the word "impossible" to the ground if you allow it to. I spoke to her about the theme of my life, the lessons learned along the way, and stressed the importance of having the confidence to go against the norm and trust your gut. A gut instinct can be more impactful and life-changing than any degree or position of power ever will be.

As I reflect back on the struggles in my life and how I cared for them, I hope my children understand the power that one person can hold. I hope they all experience that glorious moment in life where they ignite the passion that will allow them to determine their own purpose in this life. And if it happens to be something that seems impossible or daunting, I hope they can gain strength from the stories they came from. I hope the lessons intertwined with grief, sadness, hope, and empowerment will lead them all to a beautiful and fulfilled life.

It doesn't matter if it's something big like saving a life, or something that seems small like drawing attention to a book with bad words. It's all connected, and it may take time to really understand how something so small can eventually gain enough momentum to make change. Just follow your gut, and it won't let you down.

I know Ava will do just that next year as she begins a new chapter in her life, at her first-choice university. I was lucky to be next to her as she received the acceptance email. The joy and excitement on her face and in her voice was priceless. A year prior, I had honestly thought I was losing her. Life has not always been kind, but it has paved the way with hard lessons and awakenings God needed her to have. It will be extraordinary to watch her navigate and use her hard-earned gifts to make her own impact in this world.

I know that God picked me to use as a vessel. It may have taken almost forty-five years for me to fully understand this, but I am certain I finally do. I have saved lives, pushed boundaries, changed minds, and brought awareness. I have made friends and enemies, lost and gained, all fueled by the power of a mother's intuition. And as my dear friend

Candice always said, "I choose to celebrate life rather than simply survive it." She would always end her notes with "pink kisses," but I think even from heaven, she knows mine are purple.

ABOUT THE AUTHOR

Anna Chambers, a mother of three advocating for change, seeks to connect the dots between insatiable greed and suffering. She was born and raised in Michigan. She has a degree in journalism from Western Michigan University, worked for many years as a flight attendant, and was also a competitive figure skater. Her daughter's mysterious environmental illness after the high-profile death of her husband, a USAF F-22 pilot, sent her on a mission to seek the truth by following her intuition. Her mission with Saving Ava is to raise awareness about root-cause healing and the power of trusting your gut instincts.

www.ingramcontent.com/pod-product-compliance
Lightning Source LLC
Chambersburg PA
CBHW072046090426
42733CB00032B/2291